You Reap What They Sowed

By Edward J Funk

ISBN: 978-1-7320732-5-8

This book is available in print at most online retailers

Preface:

My name is Edward Funk and my parents were Bernard and Mary Hannon Funk. It's their picture that's on the cover. This is a story of a family but not just the family I grew up with but family that preceded me by generations. In the process of writing this book, something became apparent to me: one reaps what earlier generations sowed. By that I mean that who we are individually is significantly influenced by the personalities and the choices made by those who came before us. Such as owing a lot to great-grandparents we never knew and most likely have never given much thought.

The demands on parents of young children usually leave very little time for reflection. And maybe that's how it should be. The idea that two people should pair for life is pretty overwhelming if given enough time to consider. Two people, who really didn't know each other, not *really* know each other, make a commitment to shepherd a new generation into the world. And how could they have known each other when, as individuals, they didn't understand the families from which they came? So in my judgment, each new generation continues to reap what has been sowed before them.

Chapters one and two will start with Mom's family.

Patrick Hannon (1869) & Anna Carroll (1881)

Mary 1908

Catherine 1910

Evelyn 1912

Chapter One: Irish Legacy

Mary Hannon was born in Indianapolis, Indiana, January 2, 1908. She was the oldest child of Patrick Hannon and Anna Carroll Hannon. Both her parents were Irish immigrants who came to the United States as young adults and settled in Indianapolis to join other relatives.

Patrick was born in 1869, the youngest of five children. He never talked much about his family to his children, other than he grew up in County Galway, in a thatched cottage surrounded by a few acres which his parents farmed. He was a passionate student of Irish History, a history that put the blame of the potato famine, which ended before he was born, squarely on the shoulders of the much-hated British. The consequences of that famine still ravished the Irish economy, and eventually, one third of the Irish population emigrated from their homeland, mainly to the United States.

Patrick arrived in Indianapolis in 1889, age 19. The treasures he brought from home were the books, *A Poor Man's Catechism* and *A Manuel of Euclid, Gelbraith and Haughton*.

He highly regarded the United States, but his identity as an Irishman and his absorption into the Irish community of Indianapolis distracted his effort to become an

American citizen for many years to come. He was gregarious and found himself quite at home working in the tavern business. It was like he never left the old country as he spent countless hours surrounded by men speaking in the same heavy brogue as his own. They discussed the "troubles," a word that encapsulated all the woes of Ireland and, often as not, the British were still to blame. Pat Hannon acquired a reputation as a scholar, albeit dispersing wisdom in a tavern rather than a classroom.

Anna Carroll was born in 1880, the second youngest girl in a family of thirteen children. The family lived in a thatched cottage, thirty feet wide, and twelve feet deep. The interior was primarily composed of one big room with a hearth at one end and a loft above. The children slept in the loft and the parents slept in a small space behind the hearth. A big pot hung in the hearth where their meals were cooked; the hearth also provided warmth against the damp chill of the island climate. A visitor in those years might have noted the wild beauty of County Mayo, but if one were farming thirteen rented acres as the Carrolls were, the rocky, rolling terrain only made a hard life harder. In addition to their meager crops, a few hogs added to their efforts. It was not enough. There were days and weeks when they knew hunger and this raw quest for survival did not promote harmony.

Anna did not have a pair of new shoes until she was of an age to start the first grade. The Carroll children had to navigate a small creek on their way to the one room school, and she dutifully took off her shoes to do so.

At a young age, Anna took note of her parents' relationship. Patrick Carroll was twelve years older than his wife Bridget, and with hungry children, still found money for drink. Not only that, but as he was sleeping it off, the efforts for survival fell on his wife. When Anna was old enough to understand how babies were made, she concluded that her father's main contribution was impregnating his wife, promoting the downward spiral of their collective existence.

In 1899, and at age nineteen, Anna immigrated to the United States, disembarking in Philadelphia. Her disembarkation slip identified her vocation as "servant." She took a train to Indianapolis and when she saw a black person for the first time, she concluded the skin pigmentation was the result of the water in the train's bathroom. She had a lot to learn.

Her first employment as maid for a Northside family lasted almost two years, but she was more satisfied when she found work as a clerk in a grocery story. She had a head for math and could calculate the total for a grocery list in her head, but wrote it all out anyway for the satisfaction of both the boss and the customer.

Patrick Hannon had a brother as well as aunts, uncles, and cousins that drew him to Indianapolis. Almost all of Anna's family was already there. She was the twelfth and last of the thirteen siblings to immigrate and all but her sister Kate had settled in Indianapolis.

Anna lived with her family and also sought their comfort when it came to her discretionary time. And although she was the youngest of her siblings in Indianapolis, over the course of a few years, she became the driving force in all major family decisions. She had a firm opinion of what was best for them all. It wasn't so much the force of her personality as it was her strength, fortified by her deadly seriousness.

Her older sisters thought she needed a husband. She did, too. She was almost twenty-six; it was what Irish girls did to take care of themselves. She was attractive with medium brown hair and delicate blue eyes; if only she didn't look so serious!

Someone in her family, possibly a brother-in-law, knew a guy who ran a tavern on 10th Street. Since taverns were closed on Sunday, it's probable that Patrick would have been invited to a Sunday dinner. Both he and Anna would have known they were being fixed up. At age thirty-seven,

Patrick had no doubt been invited to many such Sunday dinners and probably saw this as just one more. And, Anna, aware of the suffering brought on by her own father's drinking, probably had low expectation in meeting a guy who ran a tavern.

From the beginning of time, people have concocted all kinds of alchemy and calculated innumerable schemes with the goal of attracting one person to another. But, in the end, who really knows how it happens? Who can explain the contradictions between what someone thinks they're looking for and what makes their heart go pitter patter. Apparently, both Patrick and Anna were caught off guard.

Seemingly, Patrick had been comfortable with his life as a tavern orator taking center stage. Now he wasn't so sure. He was intrigued by the crackling intelligence barely submerged by a quiet smile. Yes, he knew he'd have to get to know her better.

As for Anna, it's possible that she was smitten by Patrick's good looks. Typical of the west coast of Ireland, he had dark hair and eyes, combined with fair skin. Did she feel a seductive lightness of head and heart, apparently beyond her control? She wouldn't have liked not being in control but was she so not in control that she was unable to do anything about it?

Patrick took Anna to meet his brother, Thomas. This was something new. Also, when the couple started spending the whole of Sundays together, it probably consisted of morning Mass, afternoon dinner, followed by cards with the relatives. And maybe, when weather was permitting, some long walks. Also, maybe they had weekday lunch dates during Anna's breaks from the grocery timed when tavern business was slow and Pat could get away. Most likely, these would have been picnic lunches; Pat would bring boiled eggs from the tavern and Anna could bring a few slices of bread and pieces of fruit from the store.

There's no record of the marriage proposal, but by the time it happened, most likely, Anna was sure Patrick would be asking and Patrick knew that Anna would say yes.

The wedding was scheduled for the following Thanksgiving Day. Anna insisted that Patrick go through the process of obtaining his U.S. citizenship. He had been in the country for seventeen years and knew it was time.

They rented a house on Oakland Avenue allowing both Anna to walk to the grocery and Pat to the tavern. Into their second year of marriage, the news of a baby on the way must have been joyous. Mary was born just after the first of the year.

Childcare was probably a family operation with one of Anna's sisters watching the children of other sisters who were still working. This not only would have addressed immediate needs but it allowed the children to grow up with their own cousins, giving them a sense of family that would stay well into their adult years.

There probably wasn't a particular point in time. Anna must have been aware that when Pat came home, he had had a few drinks before closing time. She wouldn't have liked the idea; her own dad's dependence on drink had left scars from her childhood. But if she had initially accepted it as part of Patrick's livelihood, the acceptance must have worn thin.

One can imagine, that during sex, the smell of whiskey on his breath eliminated the love from the lovemaking. She realized that, even in a new country full of promise, she was reliving her mother's life as her slovenly father had had his way behind the cottage hearth.

Another baby came, a girl named Catherine. Patrick was a loving father. In that sense he was very different from Anna's father. But the drink was the same and Anna made up her mind to change the trajectory. Pat had to get out of the tavern business, plain and simple. She had been working in a grocery long enough to know how the whole operation ran. But where does an immigrant woman with no more than an eighth grade education go for start-up capital?

When a cousin on her mother's side arrived and needed a place to live, Anna saw her path. In addition to her day job, she would take in boarders, providing breakfast and dinner and a place to sleep. Her cousin James Manley was her first boarder. Within six months, more recently arrived Irish immigrants were boarding with the Hannons.

Then something truly fortuitous happened. A large home with an adjacent storefront became available at the corner of Washington and Rural Streets. Anna, who had been keeping meticulous records of her income and expenses with the boarders, secured an appointment with a banker downtown. She convinced him to lend her the money to enlarge her boarding operation and at the same time, open a "mom and pop" grocery. He had been impressed with her record keeping but more so, he had been impressed with her. As complicated as closing costs could be, Anna had calculated to the penny what she needed to borrow. Yes, he was very impressed with Anna. It must have helped that his name was McKinney, only one generation away from Irish sod.

No doubt, Patrick's own drinking had cut into his earnings from the tavern business, a tavern he never owned but had only rented. He must have hated giving up the lifestyle of being surrounded by his cronies. But he was an intelligent man and surely understood the financial demands of raising his young family.

Pat quickly learned the trade of butchering and found his gregarious personality transferred well as he charmed the ladies who shopped almost daily. Again, being an intelligent man, he was more than willing to let Anna run the store's operations; she was determined to do so anyway.

A third daughter, Evelyn, arrived in their fifth year of marriage. By this time, in addition to the grocery, Anna's boarding house operation had grown to the point that it made financial sense to hire a maid to help her with cooking, cleaning and child care.

Mary was growing up living with an extended family in that most of the boarders were related in some fashion. She was learning a work ethic with small tasks at the store such as keeping the coffee bin full and the apples shined. Her mother's hard work made her feel safe, but it was her father's tenderness that made her feel loved. Both of her parents spoke with strong brogues but Anna's could have an edge, Patrick's almost always a lilt.

As they do when raising young children, some days could be extremely long but the years rolled by quickly. By the time Evelyn was five, it was apparent that she was the fun-loving child, while Mary always tended toward seriousness and Catherine toward whimsy.

By age seven, Catherine had out-grown her imaginary friends but she could still take herself into an imaginary place. That's probably what was happening when she was playing by herself in an empty lot behind the grocery and stepped on a rusty nail that penetrated her shoe.

Anna probably inspected the situation, applied iodine to the wound, put Catherine to bed and then went back to the store. She assigned Mary to keep an eye on her sister. Things did not go well. Mary wondered if a cold glass of lemonade might help. As Catherine appeared to have a hard time swallowing, Mary asked, "What's wrong?" Catherine tried to respond but her voice was so muddled that Mary couldn't understand her.

Mary, overcome with a surge of fear, said, "I'm going to get Mom!"

In the few minutes it took for Anna to arrive, Catherine had begun convulsing and uttering a muffled scream. (Mary would be told later that the citric acid in the lemonade hastened the convulsions.) Anna was horrified. She had vaguely heard of lockjaw and now feared for her daughter's life. She told Mary, "Go get Pop! Tell him to close the store, and get right over here!"

Anna called the doctor. Seemingly both he and Pat arrived instantaneously. No doubt the doctor had recognized the symptoms of lockjaw from the phone conversation and as he walked into the room, the child continued to convulse and was no longer able to speak. The nightmare became worse. In an effort to free Catherine's jaw, he broke her jaw, but her respiratory muscles continued to tighten just the same. She was suffocating and the doctor knew she would not survive. He had brought along a hypodermic of morphine, if her condition deteriorated to this point. Administering that eased her pain but also hastened her passage from this life into the next.

From that day on, Anna was never the same again.

Anna Carroll after arriving in the United States in 1899.

Patrick Hannon after arriving in the United States in 1889.

Chapter Two: An Indianapolis Story

Catherine had been the first baby baptized in the new parish of Saint Phillip Neri, located three blocks south on Rural Street. Now she was the first child to be buried from the new parish school.

The wake had been held at home as was the custom of the time. The notion of an "Irish Wake" which included drinking of whiskey with toasts to the departed was most likely absent. Catherine's death had been too shocking, particularly for a little girl whose very essence suggested that she had come from another world and had now returned.

As for the boarders, sadness spoke to them from every room but that was all the more reason for them to remain loyal. Something in their Irish souls equipped them for such a challenge.

Several weeks passed before Patrick hit the skids; he went to the tavern several nights in a row, only coming home after the tavern closed. He really didn't have the kind of discretionary money to keep drinking, but most likely, his old buddies, in their best intentions, were buying him drinks. Anna would have been restrained in reading him the riot act when he did come home because the boarders would hear. But one night, Mary did overhear her parents arguing and she wished she hadn't. She heard her mother berating her beloved father, and then she heard her father threaten to kill himself. His words sent a chilling fear throughout her body. A few days later, "Pop's" genial mood apparently restored, and she thought back on that moment at the top of the stairs. She had hated the bald display of her father's weakness.

Anna, too, was struck with unrelenting grief at the loss of Catherine. She found that she could not go into the parlor without seeing her child laid out in a coffin. Practical in the face of her silent pain, she decided that they had to get out of that house, and even out of their current grocery, and she started looking for new properties. When their grocery business first started up, they could only afford to rent the necessary real estate. Now she was ready to buy. Within a year, a corner grocery at the corner of New York and Rural came on the market as well as the large house that stood adjacent. She went to see Mr. McKinney at the bank, and once again, he was impressed with her record keeping and calculations. She knew exactly how much money she would need and he was pleased he'd be able to help her.

Frank McKinney probably wasn't all that surprised that Anna was the business person in the Hannon family. He knew of many Irish/American families where the husband was late in marrying, but once he did, the younger wife was in charge of the finances. He had also noted that many of these men were prone to drink and might have wondered if turning the money over to the wives served as some sort of veiled escape from adult responsibility.

When they made their move north, most of their customers came with them, and being closer to St. Philips, other parishioners who knew them became customers.

The boarders literally did the heavy lifting, not only moving the inventory from the grocery, but also moving the furniture from the old house to the new. Being a fair minded person, Anna reduced their board for a month, but she knew she was getting a deal.

The activity of the move served Anna well as a temporary distraction, but it was only a distraction. Anna had always been a serious person but she had also managed to see joy in life, particularly in her children's honest appraisal of the world as they perceived it. So much more honest than adults, they would often say things that put a smile on her face regardless of her mood. And of the three, Catherine's take had been the most magical. Now that joy was gone, and her love for her two remaining daughters no longer sufficiently opened that door to joy.

Mary had always been a good student. She was intelligent and curious and craved the approval she got from the nuns by being the top of her class. Anna was too busy to take much notice in Mary's scholastic endeavors but Patrick did. As a boy, he had had an appreciation of learning for learning's sake and was so pleased to see the same passion in his daughter.

The Sisters of Providence taught at the Saint Philip Neri School where the tuition was financed mainly by the parish. The Providence nuns that taught in Indiana came from a mother house in Terre Haute, Indiana, called Saint Mary of the Woods. St. Mary of the Woods had established a school for women in 1846 and granted their first bachelor degrees in 1899. Originally, the Sisters' mission was to teach poor girls who lived proximate to Terre Haute. A hundred years later, they were teaching at Saint John's, a high school located in downtown Indianapolis. It targeted wealthier girls as the tuition was totally financed by the students.

Patrick and Anna were of one mind that Mary should attend Saint John's but for different reasons. Anna wanted Mary to have the association of wealthier girls; hang the education. After all, Anna had only gone to the eighth grade and she had a head for business few men mastered. Patrick, on the other hand, was enraptured that his oldest daughter could have the kind of classical education he had been denied by the poverty of his family and, indeed, of Ireland itself. Not only did they teach the classical studies that so impressed Patrick, but they also offered courses that would have been classified as a "finishing school program."

Mary started her high school years in 1922 and she took the streetcar to school and back. One afternoon, she spotted a neighbor man. He apparently was riding home from some kind of KKK (Ku Klux Klan) gathering with his white robe neatly folded on his lap.

Although the Hannons had many Irish American neighbors, they were hardly isolated from larger society. Even as small children, neighborhood bullies would call Mary and her sisters "Cat Lickers," as an aspersion toward their faith. In the 1920s, the Indiana organization of the Klan was the largest in the country. At one point, membership included not only the governor but more than half the state legislature. Thirty percent of all native born white men joined with many believing in its anti-immigrant, anti-Semitic, anti-Catholic message. Others felt it necessary to join for the business connections.

In part, the building of Catholic schools associated with Catholic parishes was a response to hostility toward the Catholic immigrant communities, hostility not just from the Klan but society in general. The churches and the schools created strong ties and the Hannon's spiritual and social network were anchored at Saint Phillip Neri. At

Saint John's, Mary's world expanded with friendships from girls, albeit Catholic girls, from all over the city.

Mary demonstrated sufficient competence to play the cello in the school orchestra, and not unexpectedly, graduated valedictorian of her class. But then she surprised both of her parents by announcing that she planned to join the order of Sisters of Providence. Anna tried forbidding it, and when that didn't work, tried to convince her that she was making the mistake of her lifetime. Patrick tried a different tact, suggesting that she work for a year so that she'd know more of the world she was choosing to leave behind.

Mary had her father's love of learning but also had her mother's formidable will. So the following autumn she was a postulant at Saint Mary of the Woods. The same order of nuns who Mary had loved all through grade school and high school, and who doted on her as their star pupil, now seemed as if from another planet. Mary thought she'd be prepared for this; she had been told the process of becoming a nun would be challenging. What she hadn't factored was the anonymity of it all. She was just one in a candidate class of over a hundred with the mother house home to more than five hundred women. Silence and prayer made up much of her day and was blended with physical work such as care for the older and infirm, making beds, cleaning bathrooms, etc. There were also chores on the farm.

 But the biggest hurdle, and one Mary couldn't make, was the idea that she'd have to be obedient to her superiors, no matter how ridiculous their commands. She finally had to admit that the religious life wasn't for her.

It was late in the year of 1928, and Mary came home to a big "I told you so," from Anna that didn't disappear in a day. This did not help Mary's own inner battle. She was relieved that she had made the tormenting decision to leave Saint Mary of the Woods but found her return home disorienting. It was a great help that an uncle knew someone who knew someone at a cigar factory on the south side and she was able to land a secretarial position. She was competent and liked the idea that she was able to contribute to the household income. She also knew she was operating below her skillset.

By the following May, Mary's new life, having returned home and going to work, had normalized...until May 18th. (Following is a word-by-word narrative written by Mary decades later.)

"It was on the 18th of the month, and having returned from work, I was sitting on the front porch when a strong wind came from the southwest. This prompted me to go inside. It was just a few minutes later when that wind, now at tornado force, shaved off the top floor. When we moved to this location after Catherine died, we decided to put the upright piano in the upstairs hall. That piano came crashing down, landing within inches of me. I was able to crawl out of the wreckage but not without getting cuts that would leave scars around my left eye and both of my knees.

"When I emerged I saw Pop weaving in the wreckage of the grocery before he lost consciousness and collapsed. In a manner of minutes, looters were on the scene taking what they could while Pop lay unconscious. Soon Michael White, a policeman and friend of Pop's was on the scene. The looters ran off.

"I called out to Pop, asking if he was okay. "I'm alright," he said. Where's Anna and Evelyn?" Then I could hear Mom calling for Evelyn and myself and I heard Evelyn crying. In just a few minutes, it became pitch black. We could only feel our way but we knew we needed to leave the mess and find shelter. I had already gone through a jagged window. Mom and Evelyn followed after breaking away more broken glass.

"We found shelter for the night at a neighbor's who was using candlelight. A nurse who was caring for a dying woman in that home gave me first aid. In all the excitement, I felt no pain."

Fortunately, the insurance policy that Anna carried as part of her agreement with banker McKinney, was paid up and she promptly filed her claims. So, by early the following year, they had not just a new store, but owned a building with two rental spaces in addition to their grocery. This construction, as well as their new home, was brick, Mock-Tutor in style. Ever vigilant for ways to save a dollar, Anna employed some of their customers with unpaid bills to work off their debt. One clever device was the faux tile in the lower half of the bathroom. A clever artisan simply outlined what looked like tile while the plaster was still wet.

As bad as it was that looters had been first on the scene, the saga concluded with something inspiring. Many other local Mom and Pop groceries got together and donated a fresh inventory when it came time for the Hannons to reopen for business.

When the economy crashed in October, 1929, and as the Great Depression set in, Mary was grateful that she had any job at all. But as the Depression deepened, the cigar factory decided that they'd have to lay a secretary off. Since Mary at least had a place to live with her parents, she got the walking papers. She tried hard to find a new job, really any kind of a job, but the situation only seemed to get worse week after week.

Patrick had an Aunt Mary on his mother's side who had been a seamstress at the Theodore Roosevelt home in Oyster Bay, New York. During those years, her living expenses were covered, and even though her pay was modest, she was a prodigious saver. She came to Indianapolis to live out her final years with relatives, and when she heard of Mary's predicament, she stated, "Putting Mary through college is about the best thing I can do with my savings."

So, in the depths of the Depression, Mary was off to college, first to Butler University and then Indiana University. She chose to become a social worker. Mary really did want to help the disadvantaged but she also was following the wisdom of many of her fellow Irish: get a government job, be it federal, state, county or city. Many of her relatives were policemen, firemen, streetcar conductors, and other such careers. They were attractive because the paychecks were regular, and the more of them who had such jobs, the wider the door was for fellow Irish to follow. Few Irish were attracted to farming in the United States; they were all too anxious to escape the hardscrabble existence they knew of farming the beautiful but inhospitable Irish turf.

It was while Mary was still in college that something happened on a Christmas Eve. Again, this narrative was written by Mary herself and discovered decades later.

"Depression had gripped the country. It had been snowing all day, and night had fallen quickly. Now the snow had stopped. Mama was still at the store and I had been decorating the mantle with pine cones and needles.

"Then I heard Mama's footsteps. 'Mary,' she called out to me as she took off her coat and stamped her feet on the mat. I had only to look at her face to see how tired she was. She was tired and cross. She had worked all day in the grocery store and had been shorthanded because the clerk had gone home early with a heavy cold. She scolded me because I had left pine needles all over the floor, and then she went upstairs to take a rest, saying we *might* be able to go to midnight mass.

"I remember how I felt as I looked into the starry night. The streetcar went by and I tried not to notice how happy people seemed to be. My eyes stung and the lump in my throat made me feel very lonely.

"Then suddenly the bell on the front door rang. I wiped my eyes and ran to open the door. Standing there were a man and a woman who seemed to be young, but as I looked into the lady's eyes, she seemed very, very, old. Both of them were tired, and from their clothes, I could tell that they were very poor, like they didn't have anything. The man raised his head and in a voice I will never forget, said, 'Do you have a little money you could spare to give us tonight?' I stood there transfixed although I don't know why. 'Mary, shut the door,' my mother shouted from upstairs. Embarrassed and saddened, I whispered that I was sorry and shut the door. Right away I heard Mama running down the stairs. I turned to see her rummaging through her worn black purse. 'Hurry, Mary, call them, back; I don't know what I could have been thinking of…and on Christmas Eve, they're like Mary and Joseph looking for room at the inn.' I opened the door without even getting on my coat and hat and ran out onto the porch. I stopped and the tears streamed down my face. 'Mama,' I whispered. She came and looked out into the cold clear night. She bit her lip as she stared at the walk. It looked like a beautifully frosted cake of undisturbed snow."

The Hannons didn't have hunger issues; operating a grocery provided sufficient food. And, no doubt, thanks to Anna's financial management, they all felt secure enough. Under such circumstances, Patrick found a way to be generous to less fortunate neighbors. When he'd discover that someone couldn't afford coal to heat their home, he'd pay for a load to be dumped into their coal bin anonymously. Without knowing the particulars, Patrick must have had the availability of discretionary funds.

Mary finished her studies after the fall semester of 1934. The Depression continued to grip the nation and social workers had heavy caseloads. But one thing that had improved was the intervention of the federal government's New Deal Policies. Much of her college curriculum had been shifted to better prepare social workers for service to the vast number of unemployed persons through the rapidly growing public welfare programs.

Mary's efforts went largely to implementing one such program titled Aid to Dependent Children. It was created to alleviate the burden of poverty for families with children and allowed widowed mothers to maintain their household.

Mary had been raised in a working class neighborhood where most fathers depended on their brawn to provide for their children, and mothers did the hard work of raising the kids. But as tough as that world could be, it was nothing compared to the worlds Mary was introduced to as a social worker: people, often illiterate, who knew hunger. These were people who had expected little from life, and got even less. People who had emigrated from the Deep South for jobs, and those jobs evaporating overnight with the advent of the Depression. Then there were the black families who had the added burden of discrimination, no matter where they lived. Mary's eyes were opened, indeed.

Some of her clients were too beaten down to show gratitude; there wasn't enough energy left in them for that. But many did even if it was merely a smile or their own sense of confidence that they'd be able to pull through. That was thanks enough.

Mary's paycheck spelled gratitude in a very meaningful way and, of course, she was pleased to share her earnings with her family. But when Anna decided that Mary should pay board like the other boarders, Mary felt hurt. This was her family; this was her home. So she came up with another solution. The Hannons had recently purchased their first refrigerator to replace the icebox and the purchase had been on the installment plan. Mary offered to take over the installment payments and Anna agreed to the arrangement.

Mary travelled to and from work on the streetcar. Coming home in the evening, she walked almost a full block to reach the Hannon home. About every home she passed had a front porch, and on warm summer evenings, her neighbors would be sitting on their porches with a radio from inside propped up in a window. Playing on every radio was "Amos and Andy," a sitcom so popular that stations were advised not to interrupt it unless for a national emergency. The story was built around the friendship of two black men. Mary could follow the whole storyline as she walked home, passing from one house to the next. "Amos and Andy" was written and performed by two white men, Freeman Gosden and Charles Correll and remained on the air from 1928 to 1943.

About this time, Mary endured a traumatizing event. She had gone for a dental appointment and it was not unusual in those days for the dentist to strap their patients into the chair. The dentist took advantage of the situation and molested her. Once she got away from his office, she vowed never to tell anyone about what happened while her father was still living. She was that sure that if Patrick found out, he would kill the dentist and then her beloved "Pop" would spend the rest of his life in prison.

The routine of Mary's work, if helping desperate people can ever become routine, was disrupted in January, 1937 when the Ohio River flooded. The entire river was in flood, with record flooding from West Virginia to the river's confluence at Cairo, Illinois. It left an estimated 350 people dead and nearly 1,000,000 people homeless. The Ohio River separated Indiana's southern border from neighboring Kentucky. In Indiana alone, more than 100,000 were left homeless and the federal government sent the WPA into help. The WPA (Works Progress Association) was another New Deal program, and these men assisted in evacuating stranded victims and putting them on buses or trains to where their needs could be temporarily addressed.

This is where Mary came in. Many of these people ended up in Indianapolis, temporarily housed in gymnasiums or armories. They needed basics such as food and water, and also blankets since this was January. They also needed help in filing for more long term relief. Since many were illiterate, social workers were busy explaining what help they could get as well as filling out the paperwork for them. Now in her late twenties, Mary was content with her life as a career woman.

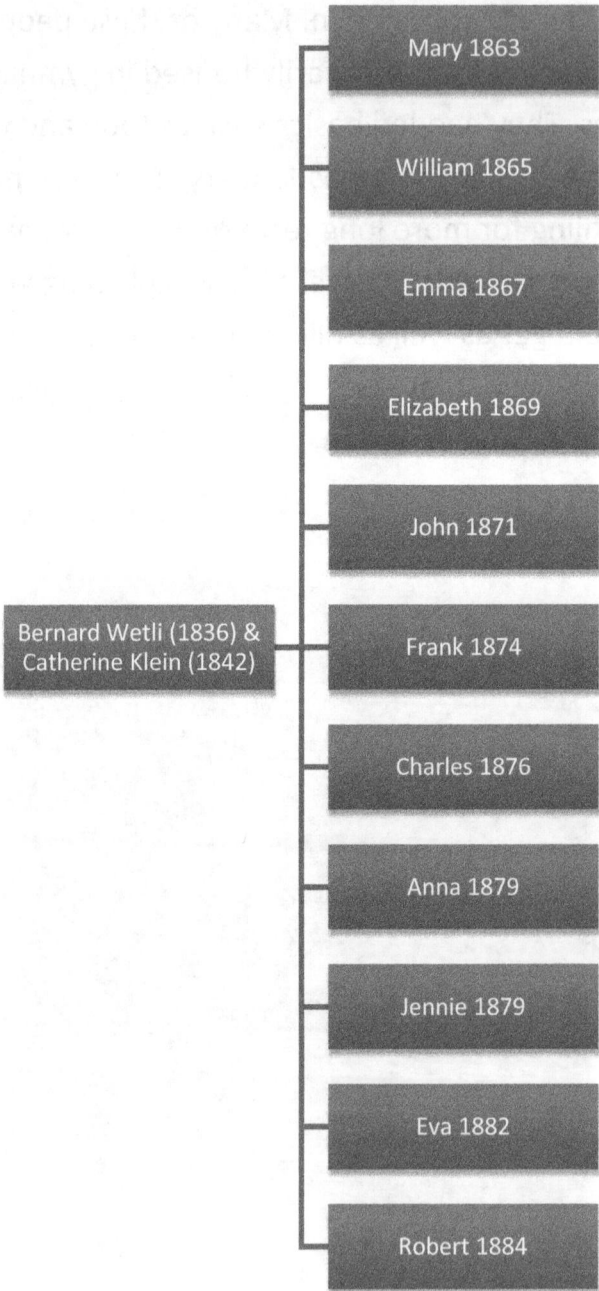

```
                          ┌──────────────────────┐
                          │      Mary 1863        │
                          └──────────────────────┘
                          ┌──────────────────────┐
                          │     William 1865     │
                          └──────────────────────┘
                          ┌──────────────────────┐
                          │      Emma 1867       │
                          └──────────────────────┘
                          ┌──────────────────────┐
                          │    Elizabeth 1869    │
                          └──────────────────────┘
                          ┌──────────────────────┐
                          │      John 1871       │
                          └──────────────────────┘
┌─────────────────────┐   ┌──────────────────────┐
│ Bernard Wetli (1836) &  │      Frank 1874      │
│ Catherine Klein (1842)  └──────────────────────┘
└─────────────────────┘   ┌──────────────────────┐
                          │     Charles 1876     │
                          └──────────────────────┘
                          ┌──────────────────────┐
                          │      Anna 1879       │
                          └──────────────────────┘
                          ┌──────────────────────┐
                          │     Jennie 1879      │
                          └──────────────────────┘
                          ┌──────────────────────┐
                          │       Eva 1882       │
                          └──────────────────────┘
                          ┌──────────────────────┐
                          │     Robert 1884      │
                          └──────────────────────┘
```

34

Chapter Three: Swiss/Luxemburg Influence

Bernard Funk was born November 1, 1906. He was the first child of Edward J. Funk and Jennie Wetli. Unlike Mary Hannon's family story, whose parents met in Indianapolis, telling Bernard's family story in the United States requires going back two generations on both sides of his family.

Bernard's maternal grandfather, Bernard Wetli, was from Oberwil-Lieli, Switzerland. After crossing the Atlantic at age 22 in 1858, he worked his way to Buffalo by feeding wood on a steam engine train. This effort provided money to pay for his train fare to Lafayette, Indiana.

Ahead lay the wild unknowns of the west, but also the wide open opportunities of pioneer country. Bernard spent a couple of nights at a tavern/hotel that serviced settlers on the move and it was there that he heard of a cattle baron named Edward Sumner. Edward Sumner ran the Sugar Creek Ranch, a spread of 32,000 acres located forty miles northwest of Lafayette. It was the largest cattle ranch east of the Mississippi. As Bernard would eventually learn, Sumner, a native of Vermont, had been in the area since 1853, only five years earlier. However, Sumner was a wealthy man on arrival and could afford to buy land from various land agents.

So from Lafayette, Bernard hitched a ride with another settler traveling west. He had learned that the Sugar Creek Ranch was located on The Chicago Road, the main route for westbound settlers. Besides operating the ranch and providing lodging for his ranch hands, Sumner also offered accommodations for travelers passing by. Many did, as the Old Chicago Road was the main trail running from Indianapolis to Chicago. It had first been pounded out by wild animals using their instincts to follow the path of least resistance. The Potawatami Indians had followed their trail. It is of note that the Potawatami tribe had been forcefully removed from Indiana to a reservation in Kansas in the period of the 1830s and 1840s, just a few years before Edward Sumner and Bernard Wetli arrived.

Bernard Wetli may have wanted to be a farmer, but during his first years on the Sumner Ranch he was a cowboy. What had attracted Sumner to the location was the thick prairie grass that abounded; his cattle had tough enough digestive systems that they could thrive on it.

In the month of August, Sumner would drive a herd of 1100 fatted calves to market in Buffalo, New York. It was a 600 mile trek and it took nine weeks to get there, averaging 10 miles per day. There was plenty of prairie grass along the way so the cows could feed. But that grass could present a danger in low areas where it was so high that a cowboy could be lost sight of. Bernard Wetli was one of the cowhands on these drives. The four week return trip back to Sugar Creek no doubt provided time for reflection. Bernard must have had a very different perspective of the United States from the time he had initially taken the train from Buffalo to Lafayette, and then by wagon to the Sugar Creek Ranch. He had always intended to own his own land and seeing so much open territory was encouraging.

But before that would happen, romance entered the picture. Catherine Klein had come to the United States in 1857, the same year Bernard had arrived. Her father had been a carpenter who built barrels in their native land of Luxemburg, most likely for vintners as Remich was in the heart of wine country. He was now deceased. So she accompanied her widowed mother and a sister on a journey by which they left Remich and eventually settled near Odell, Wisconsin. Catherine was only fifteen, but a short three years later, she was off on a brand new quest. She must have had a spirit of adventure to answer an ad in a Chicago newspaper. It was for a position to be an au pair for the Sumner's three daughters and one son at the Sugar Creek Ranch.

What might have been persuasive about her letter of application? The fact that she'd be able to teach her young subjects French must have been a plus as far as Abigail Sumner was concerned. Catherine had grown up speaking both French and German, a necessity dictated by Remich's geographical location. And maybe growing up knowing two languages made it easier to learn English. For whatever reasons, she was confidently fluent by the time she arrived at the Sugar Creek Ranch.

Bernard Wetli, six years older, spoke English in a halting fashion at best. But he was eager to make a success in the new country and very much wanted to speak the language proficiently. Catherine was more than willing to coach him and the fact that she also spoke German must have helped him bridge into English. Bernard's position as a cowhand curtailed his association with young women belonging to the few moneyed families in the area. Regardless, where was he going to find someone with all of Catherine's good qualities? She was not a great beauty, but was smart and hard-working. And something else, very important to Bernard, she was a Catholic.

Bernard was most likely a favorite of Edward Sumner as his honesty and work ethic were unimpeachable. With someone like Bernard to count on, running an operation as big as Sugar Creek would have gone a lot smoother. Abigail Sumner was no doubt pleased with Catherine. It must have been refreshing to have a confident young woman in her household.

Abigail was quite the confident female herself. In fact, Edward Sumner was reputed to be a little afraid of his wife. So when she ordered a new buggy for herself from a Chicago manufacturer without consulting her husband, he didn't say a word when it arrived.

This buggy would play a pivotal role in Bernard and Catherine's wedding. A Catholic priest would pass through the area intermittently. But Catherine wanted a real church wedding and the closest Catholic Church was in Lafayette, forty miles away. Abigail and her new buggy came to the rescue. She would personally accompany them and serve as matron of honor. Bernard's friend, John Francis, served as best man. They were only able to travel halfway that first day so they camped out near Swanington, Indiana. Bernard and John hunted for supper which was cooked over a campfire, and on a cold January night in 1862, the four slept under the buggy until dawn. After their wedding, they made the two day trek back home. Bernard was now twenty-six, Catherine, age twenty.

Although the bride and groom continued to work for the Sumners, Bernard had started to acquire some land of his own (forty acres at four dollars per acre.) He had also built a shack and that was where the couple honeymooned. It was comprised of one room with one door and had two windows, one of which opened to the east and one toward the west. There was a brick fireplace for heating and cooking.

Edward Sumner was a cattle rancher but he started to take an interest in raising corn as an alternate feed to the prairie grass. Interestingly, corn itself started as wild grass in Central Mexico seven thousand years earlier. Eventually, the Indians took notice and developed it as a crop. Bernard's farming neighbors preferred raising wheat and oats, crops they knew from their European childhoods. But Bernard was curious about corn and he began raising the crop not only for Sumner but on his own small acreage. Breaking the virgin ground, using a hand plow pulled by oxen was tough going, but the newly broken ground was the triumph of being a new land owner.

Bernard and Catherine were well underway with a family of their own. So when the Civil War broke out, Bernard paid for a surrogate to go and fight in his place, a legal alternative at the time.

After the war, a Union soldier sold Bernard his military overcoat. Bernard was very proud of that coat and wore it to Sunday Mass (now that there was a Catholic Church, Saint Joseph's, in Kentland). The coat had a much more practical application during the week. When the cold wind was blowing from the west, they hung the coat over that window. When it was blowing from the east, the coat would serve like purpose.

Catherine would eventually give birth to thirteen children, eleven of which grew to adulthood. To accommodate their growing family, they built a larger two-story home, with two rooms on the upper floor, one for the girls and one for the boys, as well as two rooms downstairs. There was also a cellar for potatoes and apples. As crowded as they were, they could accommodate a boarder, Aron Sharp. He was a peddler who made the Wetli home his headquarters as he travelled from farm to farm to sell his bolts and bundles of yard goods.

Eventually, with hard work and determination, the Wetlis acquired 200 acres, overlapping the state line between Indiana and Illinois. By 1886, they were able to afford to build a large new square house, with ten rooms, closets, pantries, a large cellar, and two porches.

During these years, they hosted another boarder, teacher Cecile Redenbroe. It was quite convenient that she was able to keep the older boys current in their studies during the months they were needed to stay home on the farm. She also taught the children to play the piano.

With eleven children, there would be countless tales to recount about each of them. For instance, John, who was attending The Northern Indiana Normal School and

Business Institute (later Valparaiso University) in northwest Indiana, joined some other students to work as a guard at the 1883 Columbian Exposition in Chicago. A fire erupted in a cold storage building and, in his attempts to hold the crowd at bay, John was overcome with heat. He contracted spinal meningitis and died a few days later at age 21.

Bill was the oldest boy and never went to school the first day in his life. He was slopping the hogs and milking the cows from the age of six, and by ten commenced field work driving horses and mules. He worked sixteen hours a day, six days a week. The triple influence of no formal education, hardly any recreation, and very little contact with other youth was bound to shape his adulthood. He was the most frugal of men and when he started farming in his own right, he lived in a wagon box turned upside down. He went barefoot year round, but with gunny sacks wrapped around his feet in the winter. He did possess a pair of shoes which he would carry along to church on Sundays. He'd put them on as soon as he arrived.

When he married, his wife Mary tempered him and he did build a home for her and their family. But blessed with his work ethic, Bill was bound to get ahead and every few years he bought another farm. He eventually accumulated 1600 acres. However, he didn't live for himself alone and did many good deeds for the community.

In 1887, Bernard and Catherine shocked the neighbors by making a trip back to Europe to visit the old haunts in Switzerland and Luxemburg. It was probably Catherine who had prodded her husband on by pointing out the obvious. By community standards, they were rich. They now owned 1,050 acres, spread out over three townships in Benton County. They had worked hard enough; why not enjoy it? That, plus they had grown sons and daughters old enough to manage in their absence.

Of course, we need to spotlight their daughter Jennie. Bernard Funk would be her firstborn after she married Edward Funk. Jennie and her sister Annie were fraternal twins, Annie being born first. Like their older siblings, they contributed to life on the farm. They milked the cows on a daily basis but left it to their mother to churn the cream into butter. Then on Saturday, the twins, transported by a spring wagon, took the cream, butter and a few eggs to the grocery store in Raub. They loved this outing as it gave them an excuse to visit with their town friends.

The cattle drives were much shorter in distance now. A generation after their dad participated with the cattle drives to Buffalo, New York, the twins participated in driving cattle to Lafayette where the cattle would then be shipped east by rail. Both Annie and Jennie were excellent horsewomen and would ride western saddle on these cattle drives.

For more genteel activities when the young women wore dress-up dresses, if not being transported by carriage, they rode side-saddle. Their brothers had built a special platform that would be reached by steps whereby the girls could then conveniently mount their saddles.

Bernard (Barney) Gocke Funk (1841) & Gertrude Wittkamp (1848)

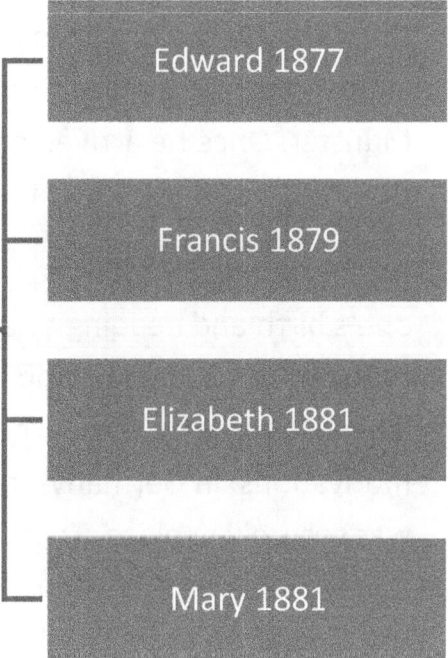

- Edward 1877
- Francis 1879
- Elizabeth 1881
- Mary 1881

Chapter Four: German Influence

Bernard Wetli had emigrated from Switzerland in 1858, whereas Bernard Gocke Funk emigrated from Germany in 1861. (The Gocke part of his name will be explained later.) Bernard Gocke-Funk grew up in the community of Norwalde, in the province of Westphalia (Germany), approximately 13 miles from the medieval city of Munster. Once he arrived to the United States, rather than Bernard he went by the nickname of Barney.

For any young twenty-year-old, leaving the country of one's birth and heading to a new country must have required fortitude. For one thing, there would be a new language to learn. But Barney had some obvious motivations. In Germany, the concept of primogeniture was securely in place. That meant any property held in a family would be inherited by the oldest son. Barney was the oldest son but his father had not been. Rather, he had been in the middle of a family of seven children with two older brothers. So Barney's dad had no property to pass along and worked as a laborer on a relative's farm. Barney was also a farm worker during his adolescent years and learned about caring for the livestock and some rudimentary carpentry skills.

Barney's mother died when Barney was eighteen. The following year, his forty-five year-old dad remarried.

Owning and farming your own land was an exalted status in the world that Barney knew. He was ambitious and wanted that for himself. He heard tales about other young German men that fascinated him. Having been prevented from owning land by the principle of primogeniture, they crossed the ocean and with hard work, saved enough money to acquire land and break the virgin sod. With more hard work they became very successful. Maybe if he went to America, he'd enjoy that same success.

Barney was not only ambitious, he was audacious. On his way to America, he decided that when he landed in the new country, his name would no longer be Bernard Gocke but Bernard Funk. As long as he was about to start a brand new life, why not take on the name of the richest guy he had known in the Norwalde community!

Like Bernard Wetli, Barney Funk had to work his way across country to the Midwest. He had heard that there was a German settlement near Dunnington, Indiana. To get there, he worked a few months on the Erie Canal, and then with his carpentry skills helped build a new train station in Logansport, Indiana. With a few dollars in his pocket, he arrived in Kentland, Indiana that same year.

But instead of moving on to Dunnington, he found work helping to grade the bed of a new railroad spur line.

 The Big Four Railroad, part of the New York Central Line, connected four big Midwestern cities: Cincinnati, Cleveland, Chicago and St. Louis. But for the people who would put down roots in Benton County, Indiana, the Big Four referred to the four big land developers of the county: Adam Earl, Moses Fowler, Adams Raub and William Templeton. They financed a 52 mile spur line that connected Templeton, Indiana to Kankakee, Illinois. The Nickel Plate Railroad already connected Templeton to Lafayette, Indiana, and another existing line connected Kankakee to Chicago.

After the spur was complete, Earl, Fowler, and Raub developed Benton County towns that would bear their names. For the future residents of these communities, the rail spur promised financial relevance for a brand new era defined by rail connections to the major eastern markets.

Adam Earl had very specific ideas for the town of Earl Park. He wanted the layout to create a sense of "big." He insisted that the streets be wider and the lots bigger than the neighboring towns. Earl Park's inception officially got underway on August 8, 1872. On that day Earl furnished a train from Lafayette, offering a free lunch, and the prize of a couple of free lots, to speculators who might invest in the new town.

Barney had continued working on grading the new spur line. In the same year as his arrival, the Civil War of the United States began and he discovered that he could make money fighting as a mercenary. This meant he'd join in place of someone else who was willing to pay a substitute to take their place. That someone else was James Wolford from Toledo, Ohio.

Barney was assigned to an Artillery unit, Illinois Regiment 119, Company D, that departed from Springfield, Illinois. He would be under the command of General George Henry Thomas, a West Point graduate. Although he was from Virginia, Thomas chose to fight for the Union.

Barney was designated to the detail of caring for horses, something he knew about from his youth in Germany. In the Civil War, military forces moved under horse power. The horses were strategic for hauling the canons and pack supplies.

 Under the command of General Thomas, he fought in the Battles of Chickamauga and the Battle of Chattanooga. Chickamauga was a Union offensive, and General Thomas's troops fought under the command of General William Rosecrans. It was unsuccessful and led to a huge loss of life for both the Union and Confederacy.

That led to the Battle of Chattanooga where the Confederacy calculated they had the Union soldiers trapped as a result of their miscalculations in the Battle of Chickamauga. Major General Ulysses S. Grant, who had control of Union forces in the west, brought in reinforcements. He also removed Rosecrans from command and elevated General Thomas as his replacement. Thus, Barney's unit was front and center in the effort that turned the Battle of Chattanooga into a Union victory.

Barney had demonstrated his willingness to take chances by leaving the world of his childhood, and his decision to fight as a mercenary was clearly another leap into the unknown. In the process, he was becoming a patriot as he shared the burdens and anxieties of war with his fellow troops. Many of them were immigrants like himself who originated from all over Europe. Among them were people of the land, and people of the cities, and most spoke broken English at best. Barney was learning firsthand the essence of the American melting pot. He liked the idea of it. There would be no preferential treatment to an oldest son. In America the sky was the limit for someone who was ambitious and a hard worker.

He was in a race against time as the cost of farmland was rising. He worked like a madman helping to lay drainage pipes for one dollar a day. Earlier settlers had passed through the area as quickly as possible. What they saw was prairie grass, often emanating from swamp ground. Later settlers, Germans among them, saw something quite different. They saw the potential of draining the swamps and clearing the grass, which would result in the residue of extremely rich organic soil. It was hard backbreaking work but Barney was strong and this made him stronger...and more determined. When that work wasn't available, he also worked as a farm hand, and put to work his increasingly competent carpentry skills. In a community generally known for a strong work ethic, Barney was gaining a reputation that demanded even higher respect in that regard.

Barney had a plan. Once he acquired some land, he'd return to Germany and marry his sweetheart. He looked forward to starting a family, an American family stamped with the promise of opportunity. It took him until 1875 before he was able to put his plan into action. He was now thirty-four-years-old and Gertrude Wittkamp had waited fourteen years for his return.

This is the account of Barney Funk that has been generally understood by recent generations. But is this hitherto version of his youth and his immigration to the United States accurate? There is documentation that he arrived in 1861, and evidence that he worked on the Erie Canal, that he helped grade the Big Four railroad spur, that he fought in the Civil War, that he lay tile, and that he was a farm worker. But there appears to be a big hole in the story of his quest to come to the United States, break virgin soil and become a land owner. There isn't any evidence that he acquired one solitary acre of his own during the fourteen year period when he first arrived at age twenty and returned to Germany at age thirty-four. There is anecdotal evidence that he worked as a tenant farmer.

However, there is also anecdotal evidence that his motivation for leaving Germany may have been gambling debts that he couldn't pay. Changing his name from Gocke to Funk was part of that same ploy.

As to why he hadn't succeeded in acquiring any land, he may have had another problem. In the next century, old-timer John Messman would tell one of Barney's grandsons, Bernard, that Barney would walk into an Earl Park saloon every Saturday night and carry a gallon of strong whiskey home on his shoulder.

It is a matter of record that Barney returned to Germany in 1875 and married Gertrude Wittkamp. Whether she had been his long waiting sweetheart before he left in 1861 is a question open to speculation. Barney would have been twenty; she would have been fifteen when he departed for the United States. Also, Gertrude grew up in

Drensteinfurt, thirty miles from Norwalde, Barney's hometown. Thirty miles was a two day trip by horse in those days. Gertrude was from a respected family and she was employed as a cook for a Duke and his family at Schloss-Haus Steinfurt, a moated castle built in the 18th Century.

So the question of whether they had even known each other prior to 1875 appears unknowable. What did Barney have to offer his new bride? Perhaps it was a chance for a new life in a new country. Gertrude was twenty-nine in 1875, and if marriage had been something she wanted, Barney may have appeared a chance worth taking. Also, Barney was handsome in a blonde-haired, deep-seated, blue-eyed kind of way. They married on July 8, 1875.

Franz and Anna, Barney's younger brother and sister, immigrated to the United State two years later. Like their older brother, they dropped the name Gocke into the ocean on the way and were Funks when they disembarked.

Barney and Gertrude spent their first year tenant farming directly east of the Kentland cemetery in Newton County, Indiana. In 1877, they were able to purchase their first land, forty acres two miles east of what would eventually become Highway 41 and two miles south into Benton County.

This purchase of forty acres brought them into the neighborhood of Anthony Dehner. In the same year that Barney went off to fight in the Civil War, Dehner bought land with the intention of subdividing it and creating what would basically be a German settlement. He hoped to attract other German emigres who wanted the comfort of living among other Germans and a ready acceptance of the language of their native tongue.

Barney built a pioneer house with one door and two windows. But their new home did have a root cellar for vegetables and fruit, and a deep clear well in the yard. Plus there was a barn, adequate for four Perchon horses and four milking cows.

Barney had made most of their furniture himself: a table and chairs, and two chests for clothes and bed covers. Neighbors by the name of Benner came to visit and presented the couple with a goose down blanket.

Barney planted roses in front of the house facing the road. His own dad, not able to provide much of a domicile for his family, had a fondness for flowers, particularly roses. Barney wanted to honor his father by continuing the tradition.

Gertrude worked side by side with her new husband in the fields. She also shared in the chores of caring for the livestock in the barn. She had gone from preparing meals in a castle to the pioneer life on the Indiana prairie. The home she shared with Barney was their own castle, and their efforts were for their own children, not the progeny of a duke.

Sadly, they lost their first child, a little boy named Bernard, who had been born ten months into their marriage. The circumstances and date of his death are unknown. A second son, Edward was born in 1877. Little Edward was delivered by mid-wife/neighbor Mrs. Taylor. Barney fashioned a bed in the corner next to the fireplace for his little son. Soon another boy named Frank was born, and he and Edward slept together on a straw tick mattress.

In 1881, Barney bought an additional eighty acres at $32.00 per acre just west of their original 40 acres. This was the same year that daughter Elizabeth was born. Another daughter, Mary , was born three years later. The newly acquired ground came with a more substantial house, built before the Civil War. It was 1 and ½ stories, painted white with a wood shingled roof. It featured two bedrooms upstairs and one down, a kitchen, dining room and a parlor. The kitchen was equipped with a cistern pump for washing dishes (water supplied with rainwater from the roof).

In 1889, they acquired eighty more acres at $73.00 per acre. Corn was the cash crop and the price of corn was so favorable during these years that Barney was able to pay off these acquisitions within a few years.

Oats and hay were grown to fuel the horses, the "machines" of the era. In addition to crops, pasture land was needed for the hogs, cattle and dairy cows to graze.

Barney and Gertrude worked hard for six days of the week and then observed the Sabbath on the seventh. Sunday was a day of rest but it could include the two mile walk to St. Anthony's, allowing the horses a day of much needed rest.

Possibly Barney's strongest hand was not farming but politics. Back then the most important man in the local community was the township trustee. It was his job to see that there was law and order. It was also his job to see that the citizens paid their taxes and the money spent properly on the local level. Many projects needed attention including the grading of the dirt roads so that they were passable. And he'd take responsibility if a person in their old age had no money nor children to support them. In such cases, Barney was empowered to give funds to keep them alive. One room schools dotted the country-side every three or four miles and Barney's most important job was to manage the schools.

German was spoken in the home so when little Edward started school, his first language was German. But as mandated by law, the textbooks were in English. This in turn motivated his parents' to perfect their English skills. Father Messman, the pastor at St. Anthony's Church, which was built for the Dehner community, demanded a certain level in English proficiency before a child could make their first communion. Father Messman was so insistent that Edward incurred physical reprimands as "encouragement."

Edward attended the Carton school, a one room structure located ¾ mile west of their home. He would complete four grades, and from the second grade on, capable of doing some farm work, only attend three or four months a year. After that, he was physically big enough that his time and efforts were required for farm work. It should be noted that he had completed the Eighth Grade Reader before he left his formal education.

As a farm worker, he fed and milked the cows. He learned to plow, schock (stack the oats in such a way to keep the grain off the wet ground) and then helped with threshing (the process of separating the grain from the shaft). Edward also participated in husking (harvesting) the corn.

Barney's motivations of what drove him to the United States are lost in the sixteen decades that have elapsed. It seems likely that he had the physical stamina to be a hard worker. His early efforts of working on the Erie Canal, helping build a train station, and laying tile point in that direction. But it also seems reasonable to conclude that he needed a good woman to work beside him so that his efforts proved optimally productive. And if there was truth to gambling and drinking problems, the fact that he was able to turn his life around in his mid-thirties points to something very positive: that the United States is a country of second and even third chances.

Edward turned twenty-one in December, 1898. To mark the occasion, Barney presented him with a gold pocket watch, manufactured by the Elgin National Watch Company. The initials E. F. were engraved on the hinged cover. Nineteen months later, Barney passed away at age sixty-nine.

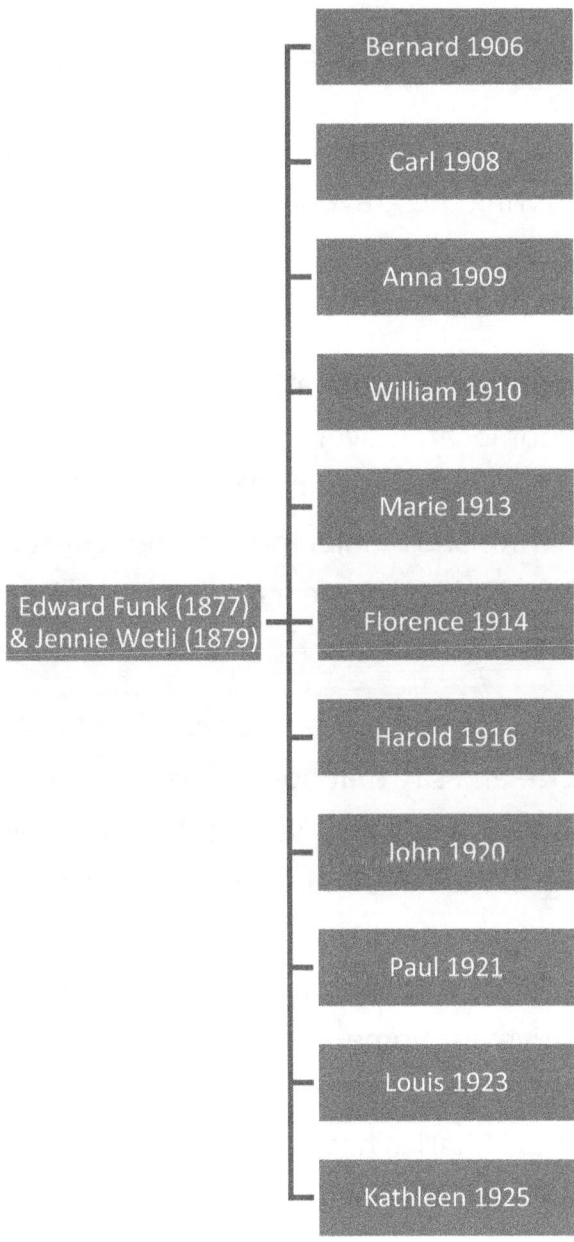

Bernard 1906

Carl 1908

Anna 1909

William 1910

Marie 1913

Edward Funk (1877)
& Jennie Wetli (1879)

Florence 1914

Harold 1916

John 1920

Paul 1921

Louis 1923

Kathleen 1925

Chapter Five: An American Story

Edward Funk and Jennie Wetli first set eyes on one another during the graveside services of a funeral, hardly an auspicious occasion for a young couple to strike up a conversation. But fate had laid its groundwork.

A few months later, both attended a dance held on the second floor located over Hackley's Hardware Store (future site of Mose Martin's Drug Store) in Earl Park. Jennie's twin sister Annie, formerly her constant companion, had left home a few years earlier to become a nun.

Jennie was escorted by her brother Charles. We can romanticize and say that both Edward and Jennie's hearts skipped a beat when they saw each other again. Edward wasn't a great talker and Jennie even less so. But the pangs of amour can do momentous things and by the time the dance was over, Jennie had accepted Edward's offer to drive her home. Her brother Charles had agreed to the plan but told Jennie, "Keep in mind; I'll be right behind you." Charles had also been curious if Edward's buggy had the status of rubber tires. It had.

The Wetli farmhouse was eight miles from Earl Park and it would take two hours for Edward to escort Jennie home. The fact that neither were on the chatty side might have actually aided sparks to pass between a young man and a young woman, shoulder to shoulder on a moonlit night. The year was 1904.

Edward "inherited" his father's farm, but not in the primogeniture sense of German custom. He had to mortgage land to buy out his brother Frank who then bought his own land nearer to Raub. Edward also built a house in Earl Park for his widowed mother and his yet unmarried sisters.

Having accomplished these tasks, Edward proposed. He and Jennie married September 14, 1905. The wedding was a lavish affair by Benton County standards. The luncheon for the garden reception was catered and served by professional waiters who came by train from Lafayette. It was the first time that many of the guests tasted the French delicacy, mayonnaise. The groom was twenty-seven and the bride, twenty-six.

The home that Edward brought his bride to was a home his father acquired when he extended his holdings to 120 acres in 1881.

Edward and Jennie's first born was Bernard Joseph Funk born November 1, 1906. His brother Carl, a sister Ann, and a brother Bill were all born within the next four years. Bernard attended the same one room school his dad had attended. Jennie had been a very good student and read at an early age. So did Bernard, Jennie saw to that. In fact, she had taught him to read before he started the first grade. He was so precocious in that regard, that before his second grade was completed, he was the champion speller for the whole school. Again, this didn't just happen. Jennie grilled him on every word in the speller for weeks before the spelling bee took place. With all her responsibilities at home, Jennie managed to be there at the school that day to bask in her son's accomplishments.

Meanwhile, it was the second son Carl who was catching his father's attention. Growing crops and raising livestock were Edward's primary concerns, and although Bernard was a dutiful son in helping his father in those spheres, it was obvious that Carl was passionately interested. In addition, Edward had a natural engineering aptitude, and Carl seemed to as well.

Jennie's mother Catherine had died in 1903 at the age of 61. Six years later, her father Bernard Wetli made his second trip back to his birth country of Switzerland. This time it was for something more than family visiting. His brother who had owned a large hat factory was now deceased. Bernard sought to claim the inheritance.

When Bernard Wetli died in 1911, the combination of his own estate with that of his brother, passed along a tidy inheritance. Edward and Jennie would make the most of their windfall. Edward was not only able to pay off an existing mortgage but was able to acquire more land. Also, it was apparent that they were out-growing their existing house. Daughter Marie had been born in 1913 and another baby was on the way. With the hired help occupying the upstairs bedrooms, Edward and Jennie and the five children all slept downstairs where there was only one bedroom.

Edward and Jennie were a great team, both hard workers intent on doing the best job possible in raising their family. But they did have a different attitude as to what was most important. Edward's the desire to amount to something and that meant financial success. He was heard uttering more than once, "If you don't have money, you might as well be dead!"

Jennie, on the other hand, had a great respect for education. She very much admired her brother Charles for his pursuit of a degree at St. Joseph's College in Rensselaer, Indiana. Edward's retort was, "Your brother Bill never went to school one day in his life and signs his name with an X. He's nearly a millionaire."

When it came to building their new home, Edward's priorities won out. He was intent on building a showplace but also to do it in the most efficient way possible. Sears and Roebuck sold pre-fab homes and Edward and Jennie chose a model called The Maytown.

Edward and Jennie's order came in under $2,000. What they got for their money included all the wood framing, windows, pre-cut hardwood floors, and pre-cut wood for the exterior siding. This was all shipped to them by rail. Edward, who had learned carpentry skills from his father, along with his three hired men took it from there. He more than doubled the original price tag with his own embellishments such as building a wide wrap-around front porch supported by concrete pillars. Another extra was the green tin roof that was pressed to look like tile. On the interior, he hired a young local man named Ed Chabot who was excellent at finishing woodwork which was featured lavishly throughout the house. The upstairs included three very large bedrooms plus quarters for the hired help. There was a large attic and full basement and, very modern for the day: central heat, indoor plumbing (bathrooms up and down) and electric lights!

The distance between the old and new house was approximately ten yards so moving wasn't that complicated. They were able to pass items out of one window and through the next.

This large home was much needed. But as Florence's birth was imminent, the concerned doctor told Edward that he didn't think Jennie would survive the baby's birth. The three older kids stood around their mother's bed and prayed and Edward was unable to hold back his tears. It would be the only time Bernard saw his father cry. Fortunately, Mother and daughter both survived.

Harold was born in 1916. The number of children now numbered seven.

Edward's lean, wiry build enabled him to be a hard worker and he gave a great example to his sons. At the age of eight, the boys were up at 4:00 and reported to the barn. Edward told them, "This will make a man out of you." Their chores included slopping the hogs, milking the cows, throwing silage down for the cattle, tossing hay from the haymow, and measuring oats and counting the ears of corn for the horses. The big Roans, Dolly and Pearl, required a half dozen ears each.

The Roans were the work horses and could weigh a ton. They pulled the plows. Then there were the foot steads whose job it was to pull buggies and carriages. Edward bent over backwards to be kind to his horses.

Starting work so early in the day, everyone, Edward, his hired men, and the boys were famished for breakfast at 6:00 a.m. This consisted of eggs and bacon (except Friday) fried potatoes, and pancakes doused in butter and syrup.

Depending on the time of year, they were off to the fields or performed different kinds of work in the barn such as making necessary repairs. Then noontime rolled around. The noon meal was called dinner and consisted of more potatoes and eggs plus some kind of vegetable from the garden. Then supper consisted of still more potatoes and eggs and maybe some pie.

What meat they consumed was either chicken or pork but very little beef. The pork could be salted and cured but beef could only be consumed when freshly slaughtered as they didn't have sufficient refrigeration.

The telephone had been a staple from before the turn of the century although long distance calling had been more recent. Party lines were the rule and individual homes identified calls for them by the pattern of the rings. Three longs and a short was the pattern for the Funk family. However, everyone knew every other home's pattern and often, as quietly as possible, they picked up the phone to listen in. This practice was called "rubbering" and everyone within earshot of the phone stayed quiet so as not to give the eavesdropping away. If the phone gave off one big loud ring, everyone was supposed to pick up the phone as there was some item of important news.

Jennie's workday was just as long, and in its own way, just as hard as any man's. Little time was allowed for her focus to be on anything but her tasks at hand. Sunday was the day of rest and often relatives and neighbors came calling. After the visitors left, Jennie would go to the phone to pass along what news she learned.

Jennie had a justification for "rubbering" any time she could. She was an unpaid correspondent for the Benton County Review representing her neighborhood, and listening in was a major way to collect the news.

By the late end of that decade (nineteen teens), Edward very much depended on his older boys to help on the farm. This was never more apparent than when a flu strain (inaccurately named the Spanish Flu) became rampant. The epidemic spread worldwide, infecting 500 million people, and killing 50 million. There were 675, 000 deaths in the United States alone.

The Funk household was not spared. First, George Hess, the hired hand, took sick, which was a serious problem because another hired hand had gone off to fight in World War One. Then Jennie got the flu and some of the kids followed suit with light cases. But the most dangerous case came when Edward contracted it, because his flu also morphed into pneumonia. Outside of the health crisis, corn prices were never higher; when April rolled around, who could plant the crop?

Neighbor Frank Schuster suggested that they keep eleven-year-old Bernard out of school to help. First they planted the oats for both farms, then they prepared the seed beds for corn planting. But then Frank came down with the flu. One can imagine how poor, sick Edward felt! Bernard went to his father and said, "Dad, don't worry. I'll plant the corn," and even though he had never operated the planter for the first minute, he had watched his dad lots of times. After Bernard finished with his dad's fields, he planted Frank's smaller corn acreage.

The Funk family was fortunate. Many of their neighbors lost family members to the flu; folks were dying left and right. It got so bad they couldn't keep up with the burials. For one thing, they ran out of coffins and the men willing to dig graves couldn't keep up with the demand. Finally, they rented a tent at the cemetery with a fence around it. The corpses were tagged and stored until proper burials could be undertaken.

Bernard was so pleased that he had been able to come to his father's rescue by planting the oats and corn, but he had done so at a personal price. Months earlier, he had been chosen to star in the spring play but that dream evaporated when he had to temporarily drop out of school.

On an early May morning, shortly after dawn, he was finishing the planting on the north forty acres when he spotted a car sloshing through the mud. It was Sister Gonzaga and she was looking for him. The boy who was chosen to replace him in the play was now out with the flu. Could Bernard still be able to learn the part? He said he'd give it his best try, and after he finished planting, he cleaned up and drove the old Model T into town (remember, he was just eleven!) He had always been a fast learner and by playtime, he was competent (with strategic coaching from the wings). To make it even more special, Edward and Jennie had recovered to the degree that they could attend, the first time leaving their home in several weeks. Bernard always remembered this as a Red Letter Day, an expression from those times that recognized special happenings one could count on one's fingers in a lifetime.

Bernard turned twelve on November 1, 1918 and as a rite of passage, Jennie took him by train to Lafayette to buy his first suit with long pants. When the conductor came to collect money for the tickets, Jennie paid the adult fare as Bernard had been born at 7:30 in the morning and that hour had already passed.

Later that month, on a Saturday morning, Bernard was to help his father husk corn. Edward was already in the field and Bernard was on his way when he heard a loud racket to the south. He thought it was a great explosion and his curiosity got the better of him. He started walking then alternately running toward Earl Park. When he got there, a big parade was in progress. The local band was playing and the citizens were shouting at the top of their voices. He soon realized that it was Armistice Day, the end of World War One.

Bernard returned to the farm to help his dad with husking. That was his particular talent. In fact, when Edward's corn crop was harvested, Bernard hired himself out to neighbors for 3 cents per bushel. Some days he made 3 dollars a day; hired men at the time were earning 4/5 dollars a week. Bernard spent some of his earnings on fancy harnesses for the horses that had caught his eye as he perused the Sear's catalogue.

The older boys all had their special talents. Carl was adept at managing the hogs. Harold was known as Champion because he was best milker.

Bill, a hard worker, was often sidelined. He was only four when he contracted a virus that led to osteomyelitis, a condition which caused bones in his right leg to deteriorate. He was often forced to use crutches. Shortly after he had been correctly diagnosed by the local doctor, he was referred to a hospital in Chicago and Edward constructed a special stretcher to transport him. Before he left, Jennie arranged for a formal portrait to be taken in case he'd never return. Bill's particular talent, one that would rescue the family, would emerge in later years.

Until the older girls were able to assume greater responsibilities, Jennie had a hired girl helping her with her unending tasks. Even so, starting at young ages, the girls participated in Jennie's weekly work structure. Monday was wash day, using a boiler on the back of the kitchen range, fueled by cobs and coal. If it were summertime, Jennie would throw her wash water on the garden cabbages, the lye killing the worms. Tuesday was ironing day which required poking the fire on the stove hour after hour to keep the irons hot. Wednesday was time for mending and baking. During the school year, Jennie timed it so that the bread would be coming out of the oven at the time the kids got home from school. Freshly churned butter would complement this heavenly treat. Thursday was scheduled for cleaning upstairs which included punching the feather beds. Friday was cleaning day for the rest of the house right down to brushing away the cobwebs in the basement and straightening the fruit shelves. Saturday morning was baking day for Sunday, fruit pies and Jennie's three-layer chocolate cake. When the baking was over, she'd go out and butcher the chickens.

Depending on the season, there would be extras such as caring for the little chicks, tending to the garden and canning and preserving. Jennie and the girls would put up over 1,000 jars of fruit and vegetables a year. The garden was a half-acre or more and the orchard produced apples, pears, peaches, cherries and plums. The berry patch yielded raspberries, blackberries, and strawberries. There were bins of potatoes in the basement and apples would be wrapped in newspaper and buried in sand bins to last until the New Year.

Making sauerkraut was a family ritual specifically requiring the help of the little kids. They'd wash their feet and then climb into a big vat to smash the cabbage as if they were stomping grapes. This German staple went quite well with Edward's homemade sausage.

With the week's work behind them, the big treat for the kids was to accompany their parents into Earl Park for the weekly shopping. Their hard efforts produced almost everything they ate, but they would need to buy staples such as flour, sugar, tea and coffee, salt, pepper and other spices.

Jennie made all the clothes, but that meant buying calico and gingham and they still needed to buy shoes.

To accommodate the whole family, they would travel in the carriage. The two horses could make the two and a half mile trip in half an hour if they were rested. A full hour if they had been working that day.

Earl Park would reach its recorded peak population of 609 in the 1920 census. Ford Motor Company had set up an assembly plant there. The parts were shipped by rail and ten to fifteen cars were assembled each week. Located on the south side of the train tracks, there was a tile mill, lumber yard, stock yards, and a grain elevator. The tile mill produced the tile farmers used to drain their fields.

As far as the kids were concerned, coming to town offered the chance to watch the silent movies (arranged by the merchants) projected onto a white sheet attached to the side of a building. There were dramas, such as "Kaiser Bill, Beast of Berlin," and "The Perils of Pauline." The kids loved watching the tight scrapes Pauline would narrowly escape week after week as her travails were serialized. For laughs, Charlie Chaplin had found his way to the heartland.

The kids also appreciated that they were allowed to stay up later on Saturday nights. It would be ten p.m. before they were home and in bed, as opposed to the "lights out" dictum of eight-thirty, Sunday through Friday.

For an older demographic, Earl Park didn't really come to life until after midnight, Saturday. Many hired men were required in those days because farm work was basically manual and there was also a coterie of maintenance workers for the Big Four spur who were quartered in Earl Park. Most of these men came from Southern Indiana and Kentucky. Prior to Prohibition, there were seven taverns going strong on Saturday nights.

The Funk kids couldn't wait to hear the stories on Sunday morning. George Hess, Edward's top hired hand, would regale them with tales of brawls and knife fights. And if you believed George Hess, there were murders three or four times a year. And again, if you believed George, if there was a murder, it was usually someone from down south, and all that would happen was that they'd put the body in a big sack and send it south on the 4:00 a.m. Flyer.

Meanwhile, Edward and Jennie took the commandment to rest on the Lord's Day quite seriously. They all attended Mass in the morning and to avoid doing any more work than absolutely necessary, Edward had positioned Sunday's feed for the livestock so that it merely required a minor shove to fall into the feed trough.

It would be on a Sunday afternoon when Edward would sit down at the piano and play the two tunes his sister Mary had taught him in their youth: "My Country Tis of Thee" and "Onward Christian Soldier." The kids loved these moments because they saw a side of their father seldom seen during the busy workweek.

In the early evening of December 31, 1919, Jennie surmised that her eighth child's arrival was imminent and the doctor from Earl Park was called. When the doctor arrived, he immediately passed out upon entering the house. It was New Year's Eve and he had been celebrating a bit early.

What to do? Jennie quietly called for her oldest daughter, ten-year-old Ann. She told Ann that she would be delivering the baby, and that she would talk her through every step. Ann was used to responsibility and Jennie's confidence was well placed. Without any anesthesia, she delivered a healthy son named John.

But there was a problem. When was John born? With all the excitement, no one noticed if it was before or after midnight. Was John born in 1919 or 1920? It was decided to make him a New Year's baby so the date on his birth certificate read January 1, 1920.

Edward and Jennie Funk's house, built in 1914.

Edward and Jennie Funk's eight oldest children probably taken in 1920.

Back row: Bernard, Carl, Bill.

Front row: Ann holding John, Marie, Harold, Florence.

Five years later, here's a picture of Edward and Jennie Funk's family with all eleven of their children.

Back row: Edward, Bernard, Carl, Ann, Bill.

Front row: Marie, Jennie, Florence, Kathleen, Harold, John, Paul, Luke.

Pictures of John, Paul and Luke in their grade school years.

Chapter Six: Darkness Followed by Light

Once it was determined that Bernard's tonsils needed to be removed, it was also determined that all the kids should get this standard childhood operation out of the way. Even some of the Wetli cousins were brought over to participate in the assembly line surgery. Bernard, Carl, and Bill weren't convinced this was a good idea and Edward had to look for them in the cornfield. But when Edward said, "Come," they came. Seldom did any of the kids attempt an argument with their father, and if they did, he'd simply say, "It's been said." The discussion was ended.

Edward worked from dawn to dusk. He would come into the house for lunch and again at four p.m. Jennie would have freshly brewed coffee prepared to give Edward a caffeine boost to finish the day. He preferred that the coffee be served on a plate so that it would cool faster and he could get back to work sooner.

Edward learned to be a weather prophet by studying the moon, stars, and sun. At night he would go outside to check the heavens; a ring around the moon meant bad weather. In the morning, sun spots were also a forecast of foreboding things to come. Curling smoke from a chimney meant a low barometer (most likely bad weather) and smoke going up vertically meant the opposite. White puffy clouds indicated fair weather while fish scale clouds indicated that inclement weather was less than four hundred miles away. Hearing mourning doves or the wind whistling around key holes also indicated that the barometer was falling.

Edward only wore his gold pocket watch, the gift from his father on his twenty-first birthday, to church on Sunday. The rest of the week, he could tell the time by simply reading how shadows fell. This ancient method worked superbly but only when sunlight was available. One day he was out in a field mending fences. All of a sudden, the sky darkened to such an extent, he could no longer see the house and farm buildings. He had been so engrossed with the task at hand, he wasn't sure if the fence he was working on faced north or faced east. How was he to get home if he wasn't sure where he was? He relied on the horse's own sense of "horse sense." He loaded up the wagon, knowing they would know the way home.

Bernard had switched from the country school to the Catholic school in town at the start of the fourth grade. Many male students of that era did not go beyond the eighth grade as it was deemed that by that age, they had the physical strength of a man to work on the farm. Edward recognized his oldest son's love for learning, even if his aptitudes were not the same as his own. He made a proposal to Bernard: he could continue on with his education through high school, and then Edward would pay for him to attend St. Joseph's College in Rensselear, Indiana. But there was a catch: Bernard had to agree that he would use his education to become a priest. Bernard appreciated his father's generous offer but felt the priesthood was not for him.

Grade school was referred to as common school. If you didn't go on to high school, St. John offered a two year commercial course. It was a business course: bookkeeping, shorthand, typing and a smattering of business law. Bernard participated in the commercial course, but because of farm obligations, was only able to attend about 1/3 of the time.

As indicated, Edward saw education as a means to learn the basics: reading, writing, and mathematics. Plus he saw courses specifically designed to learn new farming techniques as beneficial. But he did hope for something extra that Bernard could gain from the commercial course. Edward was a big fan of the Chautauqua held at Fountain Park near Remington, Indiana. He was particularly impressed when he heard William Jennings Bryan speak. Bryan had gained fame for making three runs to be U.S. President on the Democratic ticket, serving as Woodrow Wilson's Secretary of State, and defending fundamentalism at the famous Stoke's Monkey Trial. He hoped that Bernard's commercial course could help his son master public speaking, including the pitch and sound of his voice, and the use of gestures.

One day Edward and Jennie became aware that a band of gypsies were camping along the road a quarter mile east of their home. Jennie had heard stories of gypsies kidnapping children and was terrified that one or more of her children would be targeted. Edward's fears focused in a different direction. He had heard stories of gypsies raiding the chicken yard. About four a.m. the next morning, some gypsy men were creeping up the driveway. By the time they were in view of the side porch off the dining room, they spotted Edward with a shotgun pointed in their direction. Edward spoke, "I know where you intend to go and what you intend to do. I'll shoot the first one of you who attempts to come any closer. However, my wife has also been up early and she has cleaned two chickens that we're prepared to give you. Whoever is to come forward to retrieve them, raise your hand and proceed to the porch." Later that morning, the gypsies packed up and left the neighborhood.

Edward encouraged his sons to augment their education by taking "Short Courses" at Purdue, located in West Lafayette, thirty-five miles away. Both Bernard and Carl pursued these courses; Carl with a diligence spurred by his natural interests, Bernard with a diligence spurred by his long history as a disciplined student.

And Bernard hadn't been satisfied with his commercial course diploma. He went to the County Superintendent of Schools, and told him he needed a high school diploma in order to pursue college. The Superintendent told him no one had ever made that request before but he would arrange for the necessary tests to be prepared. Bernard spent the summer on the front porch studying. He tested out of the first two years the following January and the last two years the following June. His siblings weren't all that surprised. Bernard had disciplined himself as a speed reader and it was nothing for him to polish off a book a night.

Edward and Jennie had purchased their first car (a Model T) in 1917. This enabled the boys to drive back and forth for the "Short Courses" at Purdue. With a family of thirteen, they couldn't go to Sunday Mass in one car, so some would go to the first Mass, the remainder would attend the second. This problem was solved when Edward bought a second car and they could all go at the same time. (By this time, the early 1920s, major roads in the area were paved for the first time.) Jennie had always been an excellent horse woman from her adolescent years onward. Those days were now behind her and she'd never attempted to drive a car.

The final three children arrived: Paul in 1921, Louis in 1923, and Kathleen in 1925. Jennie had been twenty-six when she married and forty-five when Kathleen was born. A mother of eleven; it had been a busy nineteen years. Many more busy years lay ahead.

Paul was a fragile child, highly sensitive, but also capable of a quick wit from an early age. One Sunday morning when he was six-years-old, the rest of the family was waiting in the two cars. Finally, Paul came running out of the house struggling to tie his tie, and as he got near the car, he collapsed and went into a seizure. There was no history of seizures in the family, but Edward knew to lay him flat and turn his head to the side. Paul did not experience further seizure activity, but the family, in retrospect, sensed this was the beginning of psychiatric problems that would plague Paul for the rest of his life.

Earlier in the 20s, Edward purchased his first tractor. It was not an immediate transition from the old ways. For instance, corn was still picked by hand, even if a tractor pulled the wagon that collected the crop along the way.

There were two winters in a row during the 1920s when Edward was diagnosed with double pneumonia and was advised by the doctor not to work. Both Bernard, and second son Carl, were relied upon to bring in the harvest. Up to this point in the history of corn as a crop, the open pollinated ears took a long time to ripen. This could mean that the corn had to be picked up out of the snow.

Carl was determined to find a better way. Through the "Short Courses" he was taking at Purdue, Carl became aware of hybrid corn. The word "hybrid" came from a Greek word, meaning "to cross." The goal of hybrid corn was to breed different seeds so the offspring could produce higher yields. With his dad's permission, he started conducting intensive research, and planted test plots on the farm. Edward had one caveat: just in case these test plots were a disaster, they were not to be visible from the road. Under Carl's direction, a farm seed house was built in 1925 where he could store his corn on hangers. In a few short years, he would be selling seed.

But in between, a seismic shock for farmers got underway. It has often been observed that the Depression hit earlier and lasted longer for farmers. During the 1920s, Edward's ambition drove him to mortgage all his land in order to expand his holdings. Prior to the Depression, corn brought in fifty/seventy five cents to the bushel. Now it had fallen to a dime and Edward no longer had the earning power to pay the mortgage. There was an agent, a Mr. Keller, from Northwestern Mutual Life, who periodically arrived at the farm to collect payments. He never came into the house but he and Edward would sit in his car and discuss the matter. Unlike what happened to some of the neighbors whose land was foreclosed, Edward had managed to squirrel away a little money so that each time he could buy "another 30 days." The older kids understood what was at stake when Mr. Keller's car drove up the lane and they watched as unobtrusively as possible. The outcome always seemed to be that Mr. Keller had a "mean look" on his face but he took the money and left.

It was clearly understood by everyone in the family that they were to live as austerely as possible. There was so little cash on hand that their electrically powered house had to revert backwards to old-fashioned kerosene lamps, and, as plumbing broke down with no money to fix it, the inside toilets were replaced with an outhouse near the chicken coop.

Bernard got a job in Indianapolis testing cows for the Marion County Improvement Association. The "Short Courses" at Purdue had provided the necessary credentials. Ann and Florence went to work for a banker named Goode in Lafayette, cooking and cleaning. Carl stayed home to run the farm and since shoes were expensive, he got a cobbler's kit in order to repair his younger sibling's shoes and stretch as much wear as possible.

Luke was the youngest son. One Christmas he was given a painted wooden duck, and because money was so tight, the older boys would repaint it every Christmas as a "new gift" for Luke. This became such a routine that as he got older, he repainted it himself.

Luke also dug out a circle in the dirt and pretended that it was a racetrack where his imaginary cars could compete. One of the older girls came up with a clever idea. She filled clear empty glass medicine bottles with water and then stuck pieces of crepe paper that would dye the water. This allowed Luke to race his various colored cars around his track.

The family continued to enjoy the tradition of a big chicken dinner every Sunday and the kids salivated the rest of the week in anticipation. And since they grew and produced practically everything for their table, the family never went hungry. However, the menu was drastically altered. While they still ate potatoes and eggs at every weekday meal, now it was more potatoes and fewer eggs.

They ground wheat to blend in with the flour to stretch the flour supply and Jennie baked muffins the kids called wheat gems. During the winter months when fresh vegetable were limited, Bernard would stop at a wholesaler on his way out of Indianapolis and buy bushels of carrots. Once he was asked why he bought so many carrots. He was embarrassed to say they were for his brothers and sisters; he told them he kept rabbits.

There was only skim milk to drink; the fat and butter had to be sold or used for barter. Previously, they had bartered butter and eggs for flour and sugar. Now they were paying doctor bills the same way. One obligation that Edward couldn't barter was to pay the annual pew rent at St. John's Church in Earl Park, a revenue generating scheme employed in those days to pay off the new school. When he didn't have the money to pay for another year's use of Pew #39, the priest rented it to a parishioner who could. Edward didn't know he had been evicted until one Sunday when he marched his family down the middle aisle only to see a new family occupying the space. In shame, he and the family filed into some smaller pews on the side. However, just a few months later, the family was back in Pew #39; the kids never knew how Edward had negotiated their return.

Even in the heart of a Depression, a kid could still be a kid. One of Luke's jobs was to drive the cattle down the grassy way between the fence and the road. There was no sense in letting that good grass go to waste. Luke incorporated this job with an opportunity to play baseball with his good friend John Schluttenhoffer. Luke would get the cows going in the right direction and then run ahead of them, get to John's place and play ball. When the cows arrived, he'd turn them around and go back to playing ball. Finally, when it looked like the cows were about home, he'd run ahead of them to direct them back into the pasture.

Christmas was still an important and sacred holiday, but in these lean years, presents were extremely modest. The boys received handkerchiefs and the girls colored ribbons for their hair.

The situation continued to get bleaker. They never suffered from the cold, but by the winter of 1931/32, they could no longer fuel the furnace. So the whole family slept in the two rooms that could be heated by the fireplace. There wasn't even enough coal to burn in the fireplace. They tried burning corn but that wasn't effective so they cut down trees for wood.

Bernard's time in Indianapolis hadn't been smooth. For several months after his arrival, he lived in his car and then reported the next morning to the site where he was to test milk. Initially, two men held positions testing milk, but when they had to narrow it down to one, the other man was chosen because he was married with children. Then Bernard was able to get a job as a milk delivery man for Maplehurst Dairy. He didn't have trouble learning the route; the horses had that down pat. That job, too, evaporated as the dairy was forced to consolidate routes.

Then Bernard worked at the Dairy for a few dollars a day, and was grateful for that.

All this was happening under the shadow of the mortgage man's monthly visits. Edward decided to sell some hogs to make a bigger payment on the mortgage. The hogs were transported to Chicago by train, and a few hours after they arrived, Edward received a call from the commission man. "Mr. Funk, your hogs didn't bring enough to pay the freight." Edward felt beyond dejected; he had lost everything connected to the venture: the money for the hogs, the corn he had fed them, the cost of veterinary care, and the value of his own labor; it brought a return of zero. Actually, less than zero in that he still had to pay for the freight. He was heard to say once again, "If you don't have money, you might as well be dead"...only this time with new bitterness in his voice.

He wasn't down for long. While some in the community gave up their farms and looked elsewhere for solutions, Edward drew from his most solid resources, his own determination and that of his family. One door had been slammed in their face; they would open another.

Edward calculated that no matter how bad things got, people would still be eating potatoes, so that spring he planted several acres. He started another herd of hogs but this time with a different idea in mind. The family was going to tackle the retail business by selling pork, beef, chickens, eggs and potatoes. What had been worthless pork the year before would now be offered at three pounds for a quarter. To finance a panel truck, Edward borrowed $600 from the banker in Lafayette for whom Ann and Florence worked. Bill was the salesman in the family, and in no time, he was on the streets of Earl Park, Kentland, and Fowler, knocking on doors.

Bill's schedule was to work these towns three days a week and then handle special orders on Saturday. Ironically (given the loss Edward took on his hogs the year before), it was the sausage that was the best seller, followed by hamburger and eggs. Bacon and steaks not so much. It got so Bill didn't have to go door by door; he'd stop at one place and neighbors would pour out into the street. The special orders on Saturday were usually for chickens to serve for Sunday dinner. The chickens had always been under Jennie's province, and she and the younger kids got up early on Saturday morning to butcher and dress them.

The retail business was paying off. There would be some weeks Bill would collect $100 or more. Edward was able to catch up on his mortgage payments and pay his debts locally such as to Louis Andrews, a kind and patient local grocer.

Like most men in that community and during that era, Edward's word was his bond. A handshake was just as good as a written agreement. The people he did business with were equally honorable. In the spring of 1933, Edward sold some chickens to a Jewish wholesaler in Lafayette and was paid with a check for $1,156. The next day Roosevelt, in his initial effort to stabilize the economy, closed down the banks throughout the country. The wholesaler had the chickens; Edward had the check. Concerned that Edward would be in an anxious state over this development, the wholesaler drove up to the farm and handed Edward an envelope with $1,156 cash.

With cash coming in from the older kids working away from home and Carl's successful sales of soybean seed, Edward and family phased out of the retail business. They had weathered the storm and were on the other side. Edward had been able to hold on to every one of his 800 acres.

The sons didn't realize at that point how close they were to working together in a new business venture. To get to that, a little background regarding hybrid seed corn. There was an early type of hybrid corn going all the way back to the 1870s. These seeds, fertilized by open pollination, but a somewhat controlled open pollination, influenced size of the ear as well as the time it would take for the ears to ripen. Carl, who had been involved with hybrid corn since the age of sixteen, became passionate about the idea of hybrids which could be produced by much more stringent control of the pollination. These seeds produced more selective and high-yielding characteristics. It took him until 1934 to get the hybrids to act right, and then he was ready to go into business.

There was a corn processing plant in Kentland that was having a rough go. Farmers in the midst of the Depression were deciding they could make do with seed they procured from their previous year's crop, and not purchase that company's inventory of open pollination hybrids. The owners of the processing plant put their business on the market in the fall of 1935. Carl and his brothers saw this as a golden opportunity.

The corn industry was at a revolutionary point. But like most revolutionary points, only a few saw it. If a farmer relied on the open pollinated system, that plan might yield forty bushels to the acre, maybe sixty. But with the innovative hybrids, he might get eighty, maybe even one hundred bushels.

Bernard borrowed $500 on his life insurance policy for the down payment. He would assume the role as President and handle Finance. Carl, who over a ten year period had become a leading expert in the field, became Operations Manager. Bill, who up to that point, had been studying

Pharmacy at Purdue, would head Marketing. Bill had proved his meddle at selling when he went door to door peddling the family's farm fresh goods a few years earlier.

The company of Edw. J. Funk & Sons was born. Edward was never directly involved, neither financially nor in management. However, he was so well respected in the community that his sons knew the use of his name would provide them a big boost.

The new year of 1936 brought the boys unexpected help in the guise of Mother Nature. The January freeze dipped down to 25 degrees below and farmers knew that the extreme cold reduced the vigor of the corn stored in their cribs. They had to buy seed for the corn they'd be planting that spring. In addition to the hybrid seed Carl had produced, there was the inventory of the previous owners that had been in the seed house since the fall and had been dried out a great deal more, thereby protecting its vigor. Farmers literally rushed to Edw. J. Funk & Sons door and by the first of February, the new company was completely sold out of inventory. The boys followed their dad's advice to keep the prices down. He figured the farmers would appreciate the break and return the following year as a customer. Still, the cash flow had been so positive that they were able to pay off the entire mortgage of $8,000.

Then Mother Nature lent another helping hand to the young company. In the summer of 1936, the first year farmers were growing hybrid corn purchased from Edw J. Funk and Sons; there was only ½ inch of rain in June going into July, and day after day of over 100 degree heat. Yet the hybrids performed impressively.

All the corn grown on Edward's 800 acre farm in 1936 was to produce hybrid seed. In addition, the new company had contracted with twenty-two other farmers to be growers. Bill came up with the idea to have a display at the Indiana State Fair, the first seed company to do so. That plan was so successful that they sold their entire inventory before the fair came to an end. Edward sat in the tent with a smile he couldn't get off his face. Being paid for seed that was still growing in the field was a far cry from having the commission man call from Chicago to say that his hogs hadn't brought the price of the freight. That debacle had only been five years earlier.

Chapter Seven: Family Business

Some catching up information on Bernard. When Bernard was age twenty, Edward needed him working in Indianapolis and sending home cash more than he needed him on the farm. Carl was quite capable of helping his dad, and younger brothers were at an age to contribute significantly. Bernard had enough savings that he could buy a used Model T Ford. His various jobs have been discussed earlier but what hasn't been addressed is how Bernard spent his spare time. With his thirst for knowledge, he enrolled for several college evening courses at Indiana University Extension. Subjects he pursued included English, Writing, Business Law, History, Government, Politics, Religion and Ethics.

His demeanor was quiet so people didn't always recognize that his motor was continuously running. He addressed this by taking long, long walks, sometimes very late at night. On one of those late nights, walking south of Indianapolis, he spotted an object lying in the ditch across the road. He went over to investigate, and realized that it was a young woman. She was still warm but it was obvious that she was dead. Bernard concluded that someone had just thrown her from a car. He then spotted a car coming and quickly ducked into a corn field. The next day, he read about the woman's body being discovered in *The Indianapolis Star*.

Something similar happened when he was walking north of Indianapolis, this time just before dark. He heard footsteps behind him and they were made by a person running. Then a voice boomed through the stillness, "Stop or I'll shoot!" Bernard ran but not fast enough as he sensed the person behind was not only gaining ground but had begun shooting wildly. Just then it was Bernard's luck that another corn field presented itself and he quickly ducked in. The next day he read where a patient had escaped from a mental health facility nearby. How he had a gun is unknown.

Another incident happened north of Indianapolis near Lebanon. Bernard was driving up to the farm one night when he spotted a glow coming from behind some woods. His curiosity got the best of him. With further inspection, he discovered that the whole side of a house was on fire. He ran to the door and pounded but got no response. The door looked like it was locked but he pulled it open anyway and yelled inside at the top of his voice, "FIRE!" Just then an old man stumbled down the steps. Bernard asked him where they could get some water as the flames were still only on the outside. The man pointed to a cistern and with a couple buckets, they put the fire out. In the process, Bernard noticed that there appeared to have been kindling stacked at the base of the fire, making it apparent that someone had intentionally set it. Suspicious, Bernard asked the man if he had any enemies. The man was evasive and Bernard suddenly realized he may have walked into a situation where the man he saved might have been as unsavory as whoever set the fire. He got into his car and took off.

Bernard had already been in Indianapolis for several years before he met Mary Hannon for the first time. In the 1920s, during better times, there was a clay tennis court on Edward and Jennie's farm and Bernard had become quite the proficient player. He was looking for a young woman who might enjoy a tennis date and contacted his cousin Connie Datzman who was attending nursing school at St. Vincent's. Connie suggested Evelyn Hannon. When Bernard brought Evelyn home, he spotted her sister Mary. She was sitting at the dining room table wearing a green blouse and a brown skirt, reading a book. It was a moment Bernard and Mary would always remember.

Not only was Mary pretty in a gentle and intelligent way, but the fact that she was captivated by the printed word spoke to Bernard's hunger and appreciation for learning. But, as often happens, and for whatever reasons, the attraction diminished and they faded from each other's lives.

Bernard left Indianapolis in 1935 to join his brothers in the new seed corn company enterprise. The chances that Bernard and Mary would be reunited must have seemed quite remote.

As noted earlier, Mary was quite content with her life as a career woman. Her mother, Anna, was not. Like her sisters had pressured her to find a husband for financial security, Anna had the same concerns for Mary. Anna's concerns were seldom allowed to be ignored. There was an upcoming novena that would last nine nights in their neighborhood parish. Anna strongly urged Mary to attend with her prayer intention being whether she should more strongly think of finding a husband. On the last night of the mission, Bernard approached her and asked if he could walk her home.

What he was doing back in Indianapolis for that week is a mystery, but he definitely was there. And this time, the attraction between the two took hold. They would marry within the year.

Bill was also engaged to be married that same summer. He had found his fiancée, Arlene Nelson in Green Bay, Wisconsin while visiting Wetli cousins.

Ann, Edward's oldest daughter, knew that his cash flow had greatly improved in recent years as he grew seed for his sons' company on his 800 acres, plus on an additional

220 acres he was renting. She was able to talk him into a redecorating scheme that resulted in the living room and parlor being totally redone. She felt it important that the city girlfriends be impressed.

During Mary's first visit, she and Bernard thought they were alone in the living room and they took the opportunity to make out. They were caught by Bernard's much younger brother John as he suddenly came down the steps with a big smile on his face.

Mary wanted to know more about her future home, so she went to the Indiana State House to do some research. She was quite pleased to discover that the Kentland High School had an impressively high graduation rate.

Their marriage was held on September 8, 1938 at Saint Phillip Neri Catholic Church. Their honeymoon destination was New York City, as well as Niagara Falls. At the time, Bernard was driving a 1937 Pontiac and he was in such a hurry to reach Cleveland where they would spend the first night together that he was stopped for speeding and given a ticket.

One of the highlights of their honeymoon was seeing the Broadway production of the Thorton Wilder play, "Our Town." Martha Scott had the lead role of Emily but that night her stand-in Dorothy McGuire took over. Both actresses would make their mark in Hollywood films, but Dorothy McGuire much more prominently.

Back in Kentland, they settled in an upstairs apartment in a home on Washington Street. Both were in agreement about the need to manage their expenses wisely and that included keeping a ledger reflecting everything they bought. But not all was in agreement. When Bernard brought his shoes to Mary to polish, she handed them back.

Eleven months after they married, their son James Bernard was born at Saint Vincent's Hospital in Indianapolis. He was the third of Edward and Jennie's grandchildren and the first for Anna and Patrick. Needless to say, his arrival warmed lots of hearts.

Fourteen months later, in November, 1940, the arrival and then death of Mary Evelyn broke those same hearts. She was a blue baby and lived only seven minutes. Being a blue baby meant being born oxygen-deprived and in an attempt to stabilize her, a doctor at Saint Vincent Hospital gave her too much oxygen, causing her to suffocate.

Mary was devastated. She was now thirty-two-years-old and she didn't know if she'd still be capable of having more children. When she left the hospital, she went to her parent's home where one-year-old Jim was being cared for. Her depression caused her to reevaluate her life. Did she want to go back to Kentland? Did she still want to be married to Bernard? She went through several weeks of not being sure.

Bernard tried to be understanding but it was not an easy situation for him either. Then an idea popped into his head. The company had been thinking that they needed a farm where they could conduct their genetic research and was also located on a busy road. A farm had just come up for sale on U.S.Highway 41, three miles south of Kentland. It had been owned by a couple by the name of Hartz for a few years. Originally from California, they decided they'd love to have a farm in Indiana. They now had decided they didn't.

Situated on a slight rise, there was a beautiful two story 1880's white wood house. It was lined with federal windows across the front and a new modern wing had been built onto the back. Bernard decided to buy it.

Their new home was the carrot that drew Mary back. The idea of the beautiful house and the 160 acres that came with it was a strong draw, indeed. After all, she was only one generation away from her mother's growing up in Ireland, thirteen children on thirteen rented acres. What a testimony to America being the land of opportunity.

But Bernard had been facing more than one crisis. In addition to holding onto his marriage, Edw J. Funk & Sons had also been endangered of slipping away. After a couple of dynamite first years, they faced a real crisis in the fall of 1940.

In the initial years, the company had faced little competition and they decided to expand in a big way. They made capital improvements which allowed them to process 40,000 bushels of seed compared to the 2,500 bushels that Carl had grown for their first year's sales. They also contracted new growers throughout the corn belt in order to expand their inventory. But now, they were in big trouble. The market was glutted by eager entrepreneurs. They had seed they couldn't sell, but even worse, they owed the growers $100,000.

Bernard was the financial man but there were only so many miracles he could perform. The Chicago bankers, when it came to the agricultural world, were still haunted by remnants of the Depression.

The brothers' hearts sank when they learned that the growers had called a meeting among themselves. One of them was known for squeezing under capitalized companies into foreclosure and then picking them up for a song. He looked like he might succeed but Bernard had developed a close personal friendship with the largest grower, Jim McCabe. McCabe had grown up in Chicago, graduated from Georgetown University, and was a

Chicago businessman before he decided to move to the Otterbein, Indiana area, where his family owned a large tract of land.

McCabe persuaded the other growers to give the brothers a chance. He was willing to finance them even if the banks weren't. With the one exception, the other growers were good honest farmers, and after some discussion, they agreed to go along. That meant that they wouldn't press their claims for payment for that year's crop, and that they'd have to grow a crop without knowing for sure if they'd get paid in another year. Fortunately for all concerned, sales for the following year went well and the growers were paid in full.

With some freed up cash, Mary was able to furnish the farmhouse to her liking. She did it quite tastefully with blue plush furniture, maroon carpet, and drapes that blended the room's prominent colors. It was a decor that didn't insist on the latest look, rather it was a refined style that expressed indifference to passing fancies.

Chapter Eight: Impact of War

Henry F. Schricker was the Governor of Indiana twice. First from 1941 to 1945, and then he held a second term from 1949 to 1953. Like a movie cowboy, he was known for wearing a white hat. It was during his first term that he visited the Edward J. Funk farm. All the family was present for the occasion including the growing list of in-laws. Mary was pleased to be there, but in the quiet way she chose to present herself socially. Still, she was pleased when the Governor sought her out for conversation. They were surprised to learn how much they had in common. Like Mary, Henry Schricker had grown up in a family that operated a small grocery store. The Schricker store had been in North Judson, Indiana.

The Governor's visit was a sea-change from the visits of Mr. Keller, the farm mortgage man representing Northwestern Mutual Life. Mr. Keller never got out of the car and would leave with a "mean face" after Edward gave him what little money he could. What a difference a decade made, and again, another tribute to the second chances that America offered.

Mary and Bernard continued to expand their family. Evelyn arrived in March, 1941, Mary Margaret in 1943, and Edward in early 1945.

Mary adjusted to life on the farm and the duties of a growing family. She had live-in help from time to time such as Frances Smith and Joanne Miller. There were also women who would come in either daily or occasionally, such as Marjorie Klein and Helen Weller. Over-arching all the years was Clara Molter, an older woman who had never married. Clara was heavyset and wore her gray hair in braids wrapped around the crown of her head. She had a house of her own in town, and in addition to helping various women with household chores, she took in ironing. To walk through Clara's little house was to navigate a path through racks of neatly ironed clothes, mainly shirts. She was also available for babysitting.

Clara was particularly helpful during the times of the years when the pressure cooker was brought up from the basement for canning purposes. Mary preferred Clara to her own mother, who would decide to come up and help. Frankly, Clara had had a lot more experience and Anna could be quite critical.

Anna's judgmental nature was not limited to Mary. She really didn't think much of Bernard. The fact that he made a good living was beside the point. Anna didn't admire a man who made his living in a way she didn't understand.

Anna did love her grandchildren. It was as if a part of her that had been locked up since her daughter Catherine died, finally found release. And her grandchildren loved her. They saw an elderly woman whose blue eyes always seemed to smile every time she looked at them. The only sharp rebuke any of them remembered was when one asked, "Am I Irish?" Her response was immediate and fiery, "Get that nonsense out of your head. You are an American!" Her memory of real hunger during her childhood years must have always remained close to the surface.

The trauma suffered when Edw. J. Funk & Sons had almost collapsed from their over-production in 1940 must have evaporated by 1942. That's when they embarked on a major expansion. This time it was the construction of a six story processing facility, revolutionary for the time, built a block south of their existing plant. It was revolutionary because it took advantage of the pull of gravity whereas other seed companies were using single story buildings.

As previously stated, Carl was a natural engineer. He had no formal training in the field, but his talents were genius. He and Erwin Lehman, a highly regarded plant employee, who was also a natural engineering genius, designed a building whereby ears of corn could be powered up to the sixth floor, then as it descended floor by floor, various procedures took place. The ears would be shucked and questionable ears removed. The next step was shelling, followed by the sorting of seeds by size and grade, (grade differentiated between rounds and flats. The flat seeds would be more expensive because they would go through the corn planters more efficiently). The application of any necessary chemical treatment followed. It finally culminated in a bagging process that indicated seed size and grade as well as probable growing days for that particular hybrid.

This venture's timing couldn't have been more perfect. The United States had already been gearing up their food production and manufacturing to supply the Allies, but in December of 1941, the United States declared war on the Axis Powers and joined with the Allied Forces.

None of the older brothers were called to serve. The seed business was considered essential for the war effort and they were considered essential workers. Once again, the company was booming from their contribution to meet the food needs of not just the United States but the other Allied countries.

But with increased production came new challenges, such as finding 1500 workers needed to detassel. Detasseling had always been essential in the development of hybrid seeds. Producing hybrid corn required that two varieties of corn be planted in the same field. The rows of corn that generated the seed that would eventually be sold had their tassels pulled from the top of the plant and thrown on the ground. This allowed the tassels from the second hybrid to mature and eventually pollinate the detasseled rows. The end result was that the new seed would inherit desired qualities from both of their parent varieties.

The company had a particularly hard time the summer they hired teenage boys from the south side of Chicago. They were picked up at the stockyards and transported to a campsite set up at the local fairgrounds. The boys were defiant and managed to get into trouble constantly. Having to coax them every step of the way made it the most expensive detasseling season ever.

The following summer, the Emergency Farm Labor Board brokered a much more successful outcome. They supplied the company with boys from various counties of Southern Indiana and those boys were great workers.

Managing these wartime detasseling challenges fell on Bill's shoulders. Certainly out of the realm of marketing, it was an example of the brothers pulling together to accomplish what needed to be done.

Bernard and Mary took additional steps to feed their family. Bernard increased the size of the garden, acquired a milk cow, and raised chickens. He would come home over the noon hour, change out of his office clothes, milk the cow, and then change back again. Once Bernard had killed a chicken, Mary would take it from there, sitting on the back porch and removing the feathers. She had witnessed her parents doing this countless times in the grocery business. And Bernard's increased garden size created more work for Mary to do in the canning process. They also had five gallon crocks of sauerkraut and lard in the basement continuously replenished from Jennie and Edward's larder.

Men who roamed along the highways in those days were called tramps. Even in wartime, Mary was always willing to provide a tray of food when one of these men came to the door. She would ask them to sit at the picnic table in the back yard while she prepared it.

Around Christmas time, she would tell the story of the man and woman coming to her parents' door on Christmas Eve: that Grandmother had told her to shut the door and then, almost immediately, saw herself telling Joseph and Mary that there was no room at the inn. She had asked Mary to go find them. Not only could she not find them but there were no footprints in the snow confirming that they had ever been there. Mary then explained that every tramp who came to the door were modern day faces of Mary and Joseph looking for room at the inn.

Mary's sister, Evelyn, a registered nurse, served as a Second Lieutenant in a field hospital in England. She had crossed over on the *Queen Mary*, the luxurious passenger ship that had been converted to a troop carrier.

Kroger built a new grocery store in the eastside that managed to wipe out several mom and pop groceries in the area, including the Hannon's. So Patrick Hannon got a job at the top secret Naval Ordinance Plant. Decades before email, there was a need for an internal mailman as the plant covered 163 acres. Large blocks of Indianapolis on the east side were still farmland, providing the site where the NOP was built in 1941. The outside of the facility was forbidding. There were twenty-four hour armed walking guards and the perimeter was surrounded by unclimbable barbed concertina wiring.

The reason for the heightened security and hush/hush atmosphere was that this was the location where the Norden bombsights were constructed. This technology was credited in a large way with winning the war in Europe. That's because it allowed that bombs could be dropped from much higher altitudes and with greater accuracy. This in turn increased the range of bombers as well as giving them greater ability to dodge enemy aircraft.

The Naval Ordinance Plant was located in Indianapolis because a location in the interior of the United States was considered much harder for enemy planes to take out. But amidst such a serious atmosphere, Patrick was having the time of his life. He loved going from office to office and chatting with everyone along the way.

Two of Bernard's younger brothers were called into action: John into the Army and Luke into the Navy. Jim, Bernard and Mary's oldest boy, was particularly sad to see his Uncle Luke leave as he was his favorite babysitter. Luke wasn't gone long. By the time his ship arrived in Manilla, the war had ended.

VED (Victory in Europe Day) had already been announced in May, 1945, and VJD (Victory in Japan Day) was announced three months later. As it happened, Bernard was home for lunch on both occasions when his secretary, Grace Faith, called to share the exciting news. Everyone at the table heard these announcements but Jim was the only child old enough to grasp some significance.

It was the third Sunday in August, 1945. Japan had yet to sign surrender papers, but the world knew that the Pacific War had come to an end. Dale Jones, recently discharged from military service, had flown reconnaissance missions over Germany and had been home since early July. He was a handsome man made more attractive by a pleasing personality.

Prior to the war, Jones (nicknamed Jonesy) had been the Operational Head of the Alumni Seed Improvement Association for Purdue before he joined Edw J. Funk and Sons. With his knowledge of hybrids, he had been particularly helpful to Carl in getting the new plant in operation. He also won the admiration of the growers because of his knowledge regarding soils and seeds. But he had been a reserve officer so even though he was an essential worker, he was called up to serve in World War Two.

Both Mary and Bernard liked Dale a great deal. It was wonderful to see him home again, safe and sound. The three of them sat in the living room with the children lolling about. The two girls had been fascinated by Dale upon his arrival but he was soon just another generic adult and their interest faded. But Evelyn had noticed that he had brought something with him and she blurted out, "What's in the package?"

Dale responded with a curious smile on his face, "Oh, this. I forgot I had it. Would you like to open it?"

Evelyn responded nonverbally by grabbing the package and tearing away the wrapping. She could see a heavy material, mainly red, but also some black and white color.

She was too young, too innocent, to realize it was a Nazi flag, and she and Mary Margaret skipped off to more meaningful adventures.

Mary was horrified! A Nazi flag in her own living room! A Nazi flag in the hands of her three-year-old daughter! She tried containing her horror but was unable. Instead she reacted forcefully, "Dale, I know you brought that here with good intentions but I will not have that flag in our home."

Dale tried to explain, "I certainly didn't mean to offend you. It was meant as a gift that celebrates our conquest over fascism. To us GI's, taking their flag from them was a symbol of victory. Let me wrap it back up and I'll take it with me."

The visit was over; they didn't pretend otherwise. As soon as the flag was re-wrapped, Dale got up, said goodbye, and walked to the back through the kitchen and out the door.

A few weeks later, Bernard was again home for lunch. Usually, he would take a short nap before returning to work. Today would be different. Hearing a siren, highly unusual in a rural area, even if one lived on a busy highway, the three older kids ran to the long federal windows of the dining room, expecting to see the source of the noise. It sounded like it was coming from the south but then it faded. Apparently, the point of origin was quite near.

Mary had just gotten the kids back to the table when the phone rang. It was Bernard's secretary. The phone was in full view from the dining room and Mary and the older kids could all read the alarm on Bernard's usually composed face. He said, "Thanks for calling," and hung up. Then he walked the few steps to the table and said, "Dale Jones' plane crashed when he was checking out our east field. He's being rushed to the hospital in Lafayette."

Bernard sat down and he and Mary continued sitting at the table in the hopes the kids would finish their lunch. But when they got up from the table, Mary didn't try stopping them.

Evelyn and Mary Margaret ran outside and played on the swing set, Evelyn climbed the ladder situated between the two swings and then realized they could see smoke from the east field rising in the air. The smoke gave the little girls an uneasy feeling that connected them closer to the tension being felt in the house.

The phone rang. Again it was Bernard's secretary, and after listening for a brief second, he hung up and turned toward Mary and Jim who were now standing nearby. In a steady voice, he uttered, "He died on the way to the hospital." Bernard then walked to the back door, removed his car keys that hung on a nearby hook, and said, "I better get back to the office. I'm probably needed there." Two minutes later, Mary heard the car drive down the lane.

Standing by herself in the kitchen, Mary suddenly was overtaken by her feelings of grief, shock, and guilt. Grief that a young man she knew and liked was now dead, and guilt that she must have hurt his feelings when she rejected his gift of the Nazi flag. Even at the time she understood it was clearly given with good intentions. Add to that the irony that he had survived the dangerous missions he flew over Germany only to crash into their field.

There was another development during the summer of 1945. Through the Victory Volunteer Corp, the company had access to 500 German prisoners of war to work as detasselers. They were all high ranking officers who were being detained at a camp near Hoopeston, Illinois, and the army would truck them back and forth daily. U.S. soldiers served as guards, one for every 10 prisoners. With weapons in hand, the guards were posted at the ends of the rows.

Mary wasn't really that comfortable having the prisoners of war in a field just north of the orchard. More than once, she reprimanded three-year-old Evelyn from watching from the dining room window.

Mary's father-in-law Edward, however, had a very different attitude. He was delighted to engage in conversation with the men, giving him a chance to use the language of his pre-school childhood.

Mary's learning curve regarding living in the country continued. After Jim got off the school bus from his first day at school, a kind neighbor lady called. She told Mary that Jim had been teased on the bus ride home because he was wearing short pants and that's not how country kids dressed. She immediately took Jim to Kentland where they bought blue jeans.

This aerial picture of grandfather's (Edward J. Funk) was used in promotional material for Edw. J. Funk & Sons. John Funk ran the Art Department at the time, and airbrushed neighboring farm buildings out to make his father's farm look like it went on forever.

This picture was taken by "LIFE Magazine" in 1947 for a story on the seed corn industry.

MISS EXECUTIVE SECRETARY OF 1948

VOTE FOR

KATHY FUNK

This picture was taken while Kathleen, Edward and Jennie's youngest child, was attending Indiana University Business School.

Back row: Bill, Carl, Paul, John, Bernard, Harold, Luke.

Middle row: Kathleen, Florence, Ann, Marie.

Front: Jennie and Edward.

The old seed house in flames,
September, 1949.

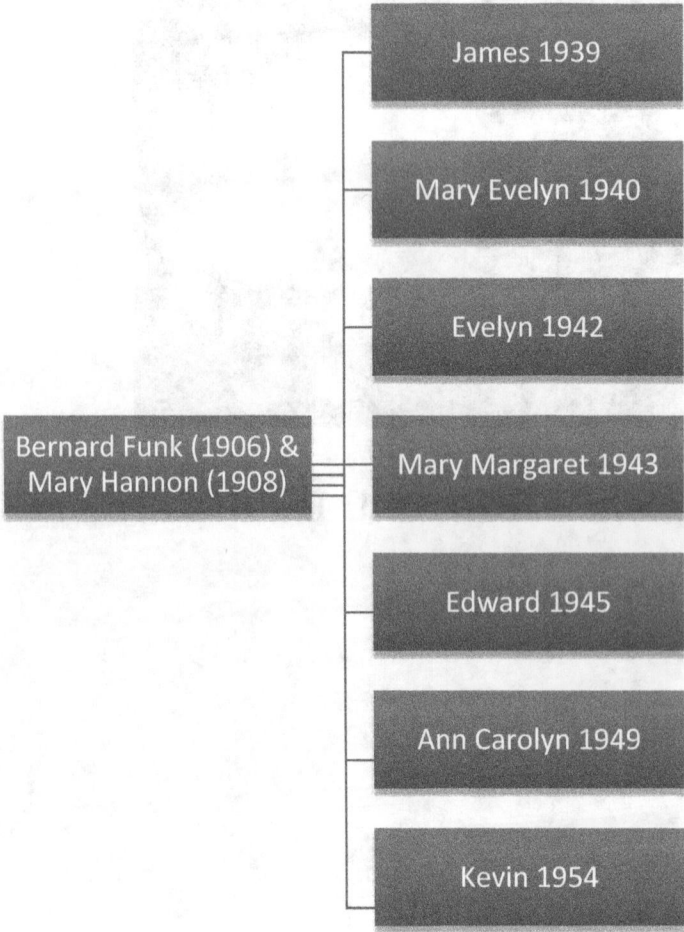

Bernard Funk (1906) & Mary Hannon (1908)

James 1939

Mary Evelyn 1940

Evelyn 1942

Mary Margaret 1943

Edward 1945

Ann Carolyn 1949

Kevin 1954

Chapter Nine: New Decade, New Crisis

Bernard's quest for knowledge had continued. The family's set of encyclopedias was well utilized as he read through every volume, page by page. That took more than a year. Then he started on page one of the dictionary and read it through, a couple of pages each evening. For the rest of his life, he would have such a love for words that he could identify almost every word's etymology including what country it originated.

All of this was part of Bernard's nighttime reading and thus, that was how he was engaged when the little kids came in for their bedtime hugs. In the master bedroom, there was a double bed in which Mary slept and, divided by a night table, a single bed for Bernard. Bernard would put his book down long enough for the hugs, and while giving them, uttered sounds like soothing grunts. Mary didn't give nighttime hugs, or for that matter, she didn't give hugs period. The kids never gave it a thought because that's the way it had always been.

Mary was also a voracious reader and one time stated that she had read every book in the Kentland library worth reading. She belonged to a book club and participated in a study club affiliated with the parish. Her work with the National Council of Catholic Women would eventually merit her placement in "Who's Who in American Women."

On the business front, Bill was creating new opportunities. He formed a relationship with Charlie Halleck. Halleck was not only a United States Congressman from Indiana's Second District, but from 1946 to 1952, was the Majority Leader of the House. It was during these years that the Marshall Plan, also known as the European Recovery Program, was instigated to provide aid to Western Europe following the devastation of World War Two. This meant supplying food and other necessities. One of those necessities was hybrid seed corn and Halleck helped the company become a supplier.

On another front, Bill put forth a program by which the company could build stronger relationships with the customers. Traditionally, the word "vacation" was not in a farmer's vocabulary. But post war, farmers began to specialize and for grain farmers, there was some discretionary time. The concept of incentive travel was first initiated with a fishing trip to Forest Lodge in Northern Wisconsin. The feedback was very encouraging so they repeated the venture the following summer.

Not only did it allow the company to sell itself on a deeper level with the customers, but what had become quite apparent, the customers were bonding with each other.

Bill decided that it could even work on a higher level if wives could also be included.

He learned that a hunting lodge was for sale on Lake Gogebic in the wilderness of the Upper Peninsula of Michigan. Built in 1924 by timber baron Bill Bonifas, it was surrounded by a mile long frontage and 160 acres of hardwood timber. The lodge was three stories high, had a ballroom on the second floor, and was completely furnished. The 30X50 foot living room was centered by an inviting stone fireplace, and groupings of leather furniture were set throughout the room.

Boniface lived long enough to entertain Henry Ford at his lodge but died soon thereafter. So, prior to the time the seed company was looking at the property, there had been no guests there for several years.

The question was: would farmers think it was too grand? Bill concluded that they wouldn't since they now would be bringing their wives along. So, in short order, guest cabins were built, along with tennis courts, croquet courts, and horseshoe courts.

Deer were running all over the place, and if you wanted to see bear, all you had to do was drive to the garbage dump at dusk.

What did Edward think about the idea of selling corn by entertaining dealers at the fancy lodge? He and Jennie both contributed to its success. Jennie fell back on the talents she displayed as a young girl and played the appropriate chords for square dancing. Edward's contribution was less visible but just as appreciated. He supplied the prime beef from his herd of fat, white-faced Herefords. Edward didn't charge for these provisions; it was just family helping out family.

Sisters Ann and Marie had worked in the office since the business began, but during the season, Ann lived up north and assumed day-by-day operations of the lodge.

It was while managing the lodge that Ann became engaged to Harvey Sparks. He was Canadian by birth and the kind of guy who could fix anything from a leaky faucet to a jammed typewriter. As they were planning their wedding, including Harvey participating in sessions to convert to Catholicism, Harvey was making other plans. Just two weeks before the wedding, Harvey was able to get his hands on several thousand dollars of Ann's money and took off with her Buick. It seems that Harvey was intent on marrying another woman back in Canada. It was his sister who called to reveal his duplicity, and Harvey was captured while still in Michigan. Ann chose not to press charges if the money and car were returned. She wanted to get the incident behind her as quickly as possible.

Patrick Hannon had been diagnosed with heart disease and in the summer of 1947, he fell into a quick decline. Mary never really lost the closeness she felt toward her father since childhood, and spent as much time with him as possible during his final weeks. Live-in helper, Frances Smith, could keep an eye on the three oldest children but Mary took eighteen-month-old Edward with her to Indianapolis. Patrick's bed had been moved to the dining room and that's also where Mary placed Edward's crib. On the days he was capable, Patrick found his grandson's antics entertaining.

After a couple of weeks, Patrick appeared to be rallying, and Mary decided it would be a good time to return to the farm to check on the older kids. That night she was in bed when the upstairs phone rang around 11:00 p.m. It was her sister Evelyn calling to tell her that Patrick had passed away.

Mary was grief stricken, but she also felt so guilty that she hadn't been with her dad in his final moments. Suddenly, she was enveloped with a fear that when her own end came, that she would die alone. It was at that moment she heard her father's voice telling her tenderly in the

Irish brogue (that he had never lost) "Don't worry, Mary. I'll be with you."

Bernard had a thing about honesty. From the window of his office in the old seed-house, he began noticing a pattern regarding a certain state trooper. It appeared that if the trooper was following a junk car going over the speed limit, he would bring him back to face the Justice of the Peace. If he had followed an expensive car going over the speed limit, the trooper returned to town alone. Bernard concluded that the trooper was taking bribes and he started keeping a ledger of the cars and the dates of the activity he was observing.

He asked the trooper to come to his office and when he did, Bernard accused the trooper of taking bribes. The trooper declared, "You're crazy. I've never done anything like that in my life." Then Bernard presented the ledger he had been keeping and said, "And I know exactly who I should show this to."

The trooper broke down, pleading that he had a family to support. And if Bernard would keep his ledger to himself, he'd never again take another bribe. Bernard agreed but added, "I'll continue to keep my eyes open."

Bernard had such a good reputation that the movers and shakers in the Democratic Party of Benton County thought he'd be an excellent candidate for Governor. That dream faded quickly once they realized how much money they'd need to raise.

Even after Carl's new plant became operational in the early forties, the company offices remained in the original seed-house that was bought in 1935. Fourteen years later, September 1949, Bill was working late in his office. It wasn't unusual for Bill to be working late. His brain was always going full speed as he came up with new sale's promotions and he would need to work out the details before communicating his ideas to others.

He heard a rat-tat-tat sound and identified it as the venetian blind banging against the window. He thought it strange but left his office at 9:30 p.m. His home phone rang at 3:45 a.m. The local operator was calling to tell him that the seed-house was on fire.

What had happened was that a distorted bearing in a sheller dryer overheated and caught fire. Within minutes, the building was in flames that darted fifty feet into the sky. What had caused the venetian blind to hit the window earlier was the vibration of the distorted bearing. The fire burned for over a week causing over $200,000.00 in damage. Fortunately, insurance helped the brothers to recoup enough of their losses that they could continue in business.

There was no insurance for the trouble the company found itself in two years later. At issue was the value of inventory carried over into a following year. In reality, that seed did not hold its value so Bernard went to Washington, D.C. (his first trip there) to talk with the Internal Revenue. Through the intercession of a local Congressman he was able to meet with someone with authority and was given permission to re-compute the carry-over inventory. Bernard asked him to send a letter in writing and the IRS guy said that the letter would need to come from his boss but he would see that he got it.

A few years went by and the company used the new method of computation. Uncharacteristic of his cautious nature, Bernard had forgotten about the letter that never came. Then in the summer of 1951, came a demand for $100,000 in back taxes plus an additional fine culminating in a law suit. Bernard could face prison time as well.

Bernard contacted the IRS man who had given him permission but that man now claimed no memory of the meeting and no memory of granting permission. The company would not have been able to absorb such a loss so it would bring an end to Edw. J. Funk & Sons.

The trial was held in the Federal Count in Hammond, Indiana. Bernard took a look at the jury and was not encouraged. The ten small businessmen didn't look a bit sympathetic with a guy who hadn't paid up, especially such a large sum. However, Bernard's Chicago attorney thought he saw a glimmer of hope with one of the two women jurors. Maybe she'd believe Bernard's story: that he was being tried over a technicality, and that he was, at heart, an honest farm boy.

Just three months earlier, Bernard had completed a three year law course through LaSalle Extension, a correspondence school in Chicago. Bernard had whizzed through the program in thirteen months. After two days of testimony, a verdict was due the following day. That night, Bernard thought he remembered something that might help him out. He read through the night and found in an old law book a statute that, under certain circumstances, the accused could go before the jury and plead his case in private. Just the accused present, no judge, no lawyers.

The next day he brought the statute book with him. His lawyer had never heard of such a thing nor had the judge, but when the judge looked at it, he concluded that the case in hand fell under the certain circumstances and that such action could be taken.

The judge allowed Bernard twenty minutes in the jury room to make his case. Bernard told the jury that he had received permission from Washington Tax Officials but then they later reneged and that was how he had gotten into such a mess.

It was a hung jury and Bernard was pretty sure that it was that one woman that saved his hide.

Bernard returned to Kentland breathing a sigh of relief. A couple weeks later, the Chicago lawyer called. He had the head tax man for the Middlewest in his office with a proposition. All Bernard had to do to insure that the government didn't attempt to retry was to grease the guy's hand with $10,000.00. Bernard said that the guy could go to hell.

A few months later, the Chicago lawyer called again. He asked Bernard if he had seen "The Chicago Tribune" that morning.

Bernard replied, "Not yet."

"Hurry and look," said the lawyer.

Bernard did look and there on the front page was a featured article. The byline read, "Tax Man Goes to Jail," with the lead sentence reading, "President Truman puts head of tax collections in Midwest jail." So the guy who was going to put Bernard behind bars ended up there himself!

Bill had managed a couple of major public relations coups in the late 40s. He managed to convince "Life Magazine" to do a story on the company to be utilized in their science section. The focus would be on the "what and why" of the detasseling program. His youngest sister Kathleen was a real looker and he almost landed her on the cover of the issue before the magazine retreated from giving Edw. J. Funk and Sons so much free publicity. They ended up using a picture of a painting of Madame Du Barry, which must have left a lot of readers scratching their heads.

Just a few months later, when Edward turned seventy, Bill had scored a write-up in "The Chicago Tribune." Imagine Edward's delight to read an article about himself and his family in the paper he had read daily all his life.

The article began with, "Kentland, Indiana. When Edward J. Funk celebrates his 70th birthday tomorrow, the group gathered at the Funk farm near here will represent a unique and successful business organization as well as a large Indiana family.

"Funk has seven sons and four daughters, and all except one of the children are engaged in the hybrid corn seed producing business. Their organization involves more than farming. The company has 125 permanent employees engaged in production and selling, augmented during the midsummer growing season by as many as 1,000 employees, mostly school children and 4-H club members, who detassel the corn in the fields. Its dealer organization spreads throughout the corn belt states." The article goes on to mention how the various sons and daughters were engaged in the business.

The byline of the article read: "This Business is Just a Big Happy Family." Perhaps a more truthful byline might have read: "Family Business Still Holding it Together." And they would for another twenty years as long as Edward was still living and the next generation wasn't battling for position. This should not be so surprising. All families suffer tensions, all the more so when their their livelihoods are intertwined.

But, as the 1950s moved along, all seemed well enough. Edward was still farming, but he had plenty of help. Like his dad before him, he had a love of flowers but rather than just some rose bushes, he had a formal flower garden just south of the house. It was a rectangle made up of four flower beds divided by grass walkways. In the center was a birdbath surrounded by red canna lilies.

Jennie's life, too, was much calmer and she also had help in maintaining their large home. The kitchen had been remodeled a couple of times over the years but in addition to a modern stove, she held onto the stove that was fueled by corn cobs. For decades, she had been renowned for her angel food cake, and the only way she felt confident of success was to use a recipe that called for the exact number of cobs to be burned.

Bernard and Mary's family had grown to five children when Carolyn arrived in February, 1949. They would expand their family one more time when Kevin was born in January, 1954. Mary was age forty-six at the time and Kevin's presence would keep both his parents young well into their sixties.

Bernard Funk (1906) &
Mary Hannon (1908)

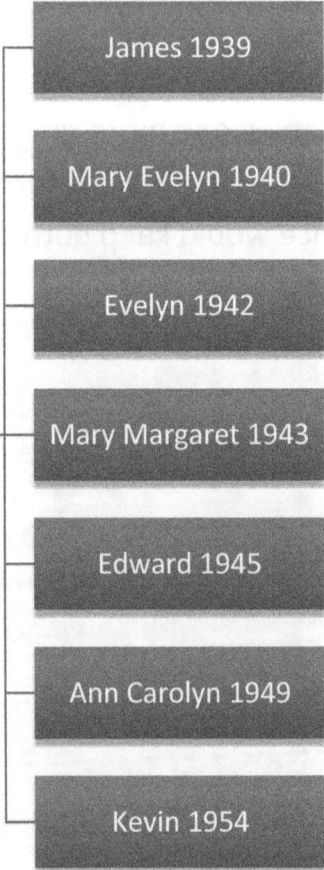

James 1939

Mary Evelyn 1940

Evelyn 1942

Mary Margaret 1943

Edward 1945

Ann Carolyn 1949

Kevin 1954

Bernard and Mary Funk's farmhouse in the 1950s.

Bernard and Mary Funk's family. Although the text of this book ends in the early 1950s, this picture is from the late 1950s so that Kevin could be included.

Back row: Mary Margaret, Edward, Jim, Evelyn, Carolyn.

Front row: Mary, Kevin, Bernard.

Epilogue

If you are part of the family recorded in this book, it is my hope that, as you read it, you recognized some traits of family members you know, or have known, as having been present to those from earlier generations. I'm not suggesting that our lives are pre-destined by these earlier generations. Rather, among all the choices that we make, there are also forces present of which we're not aware. As Nancy Dallaville of Fairfield University writes, "The generations that go before us lives anew in the fragile moments of our lives."

Acknowledgments:

Thank you to:

William E. Funk for his informative books "Bring on the Future" and "Sod, Seed, and Sacrifice," Ann Funk D'Antonio for her incalculable contribution by compiling the Wetli and Funk family tree books, memoir of Mary Scheetz, writings of Gertrude Datzman, Indianapolis history consultant Tim Arvin, Benton County Historical Society, The Earl Park Centennial Book, and the Mormon Library, Los Angeles.

Oral histories of Bernard Funk, Mary Hannon Funk, James Funk, Evelyn Funk Friedman, Sister Mary Margaret Funk, O.S.B., Carolyn Funk Benner, John R. Funk, Luke Funk, and Patricia Funk.

Kevin Funk, for alerting me that there were two volumes of essays written by our father, Bernard Funk. Dad wrote these while taking creative writing classes at Purdue after his retirement. The volumes constituted seven hundred pages, and once I got into them, I realized that I would need to start this project over again. So, more than anyone, I wish to thank Dad for the treasure trove his writings produced.

To my sister, Carolyn Benner, who served as editor, to Anji Strasburger, who served as copy editor, and to Todd Hipsher, who helped me with every techy aspect of writing and publishing this book.

www.ingramcontent.com/pod-product-compliance
Lightning Source LLC
LaVergne TN
LVHW021347080426
835508LV00020B/2151